David –

   We now realize
that you've been
holding out on us –
you're an expert!

     Have fun!

     Love,
      K & R

LIFE SENTENCE

THE GUY'S SURVIVAL GUIDE
TO GETTING ENGAGED
AND MARRIED

J. D. SMITH

WARNER BOOKS

A Time Warner Company

Warner Books, Inc., 1271 Avenue of the Americas, New York, NY 10020
Visit our Web site at www.warnerbooks.com

A Time Warner Company
Printed in the United States of America

First Printing: June 1999

10 9 8 7 6 5 4 3 2

Library of Congress Cataloging-in-Publication Data
Smith, J. D. (Jeffrey Duke)
    Life sentence : the guy's survival guide to getting engaged and married / J. D. Smith.
        p.   cm.
    ISBN 0-446-67430-3
    1. Marriage—Humor. 2. Wives—Humor. 3. Man-woman relationships—Humor.
    I. Title.
    PN6231.M3S47   1999
    818'.5407—dc21   98-49356
                                                                          CIP

Book design and text composition by Lili Schwartz
Cover design and illustration by Lou Brooks

TO MY FRIENDS,
WHOSE NAMES HAVE BEEN CHANGED.
YOU KNOW WHO YOU ARE.

CONTENTS

THE BOOK THEY DON'T WANT YOU TO READ

"Marriage is the triumph of hope over experience."
—**SAMUEL JOHNSON**

I was sitting on a chairlift one day last winter with a married friend and another guy from the singles line. My friend started telling me one of those "You'll never believe what my wife did" kind of stories about married life. When he was done, the other guy, a total stranger, jumped in and said, "Not you, too? I thought I was the only one!" They started talking across me, really getting into it, trying to top each other's last offer. "I'll see your wife and raise you one."

They couldn't believe how remarkably similar, how universally true their experiences were. Each story resonated. They were equally surprised that no one had taken them aside and explained all of this—any of this—to them before they took that long walk down the aisle to say the two little words that would change their lives forever. That's when the other guy said, "Somebody should write a book about all this shit."

It seems hard to imagine that there isn't more readily accessible advice for grooms-to-be. This may be the only topic under the sun with no dedicated Web site. Nobody told the betrothed that this was the deal. Just hearing that there was no "Son, you're old enough now to know this..." speech was like an alarm going off in my head. I want to know this stuff before I tie the knot. My friends are intelligent people, so seeing them flying blind into probably the biggest decision of their life was like seeing a good actor in a bad straight-to-video movie—did they read the script before they signed the contract?

This book begins after a lot has already happened. We open after Boy Meets Girl; after Boy Gets Girl; Boy Loses Girl; Girl Tortures Boy; Boy Begs Girl; and Boy Gets Girl Back. We will skip past most of the first act and some of the second, which in most cases means Boy Sleeps with Girl, and we will jump off at the point where Boy Wants to Marry Girl.

You, Boy, already know a lot about her, Girl. You know—and presumably like—her sense of humor, values, the way she kisses and does a lot of other things. You certainly have had your share of disagreements, even a handful of knock-down, drag-out, call-in-the-cavalry fights. You may have even been to couples counseling to deal with any of a long list of problems that she has with you, Boy. Nevertheless, here you stand, ready to end it all and get married.

This book is for any man who is getting, thinking about getting, knows someone who is getting, or is recently married. You are my friends, comrades, brothers in arms. I will undertake this mission to give you a chance to see what you have to look forward to—for better and worse, till death do you part. A few myths will be debunked, a few truths laid bare, some lamentable facts explained. If you read carefully, you may be able to see the warning signs. Guys who have been married eight years or more don't need this book. They know it backwards and forwards. It's yesterday's news. They've lived every word of it. They've been through the wars. They've won a few and lost a few, but they're still standing.

A few women might buy this book although they are expressly not invited. Typical. I refer you to Eve and Pandora. They just can't leave well enough alone. Didn't we let you have your own section of the bookstore, no questions asked? Curiosity killed the cat, you know. (Yes, but satisfaction brought her back, I can hear you purring.) I strongly suspect that women will not like this book, will strongly disagree with parts of it, and will not think it is one bit funny. Here's a joke: Why do women fake orgasms? Because they think we care. Who cares if you hate this book? Who asked you? Get your own damn book.

Maybe you think you've got the perfect woman. You think you don't need this book and its relentlessly sarcastic tone. You think she's going to act like your adoring girlfriend for the next hundred years. The wedding will not be a stressful experience. The transition to husband and wife will be seamless. Your sex life is going to continue pretty much the same as ever. Children won't stress you out. There won't be any money issues to deal with. Life will be one long dreamy experience. In which case you are dismissed. You're free to go now and live happily ever after. Go on, get out. Don't come crawling back to me in a year or five or ten, crying about how you should've just read the goddamn book and everything would have been different. How you were blindsided by your perfect angel when she asked for a divorce on the grounds of "incompatibility" (see "Compatibility"). Skip ahead to the chapter titled "Your Second Wife," and work your way backwards, hotshot.

You will look back in hindsight and realize that nobody gave you any good advice about getting married or what to expect afterwards.

Maybe there is no such thing as good advice because one must intimately know the psychotic mess you're dealing with. Marriage is one long tap dance. You're going to have to wing it. Jump into the deep end of the pool and swim as fast as you can. You'll wake up ten years later and say, "What the fuck was that all about?"

My friend Charlie called to say that this is the most subversive book since *The Anarchist Cookbook*. Men have fought and killed and died to attain this information. If women get ahold of it and our few precious little secrets are out there laid bare before the world, we are finished as a race, or sex, or whatever we are.

What's at stake here is nothing less than the future of civilization itself. Listen, you big dummy: Women are gunning for you. The fair sex has declared you fair game. They've got a plan: Rope you in with their feminine wiles, then make you fall in love. Then, only after you're on the hook, they let you have it. It's like an emotional pyramid scheme.

We, in contrast, don't have a clue. Did you ever take a class in high school, maybe a foreign language, where you just didn't "get it"? At the time you might have thought you were the only one, but if you actually asked anyone else in the class they would have told you that they didn't "get it" either. Such is life. It was ever thus.

The reason we are clueless is the result of a conspiracy to suppress the information contained in this book. A conspiracy on a par with the Illuminati or the Trilateral Commission. It makes the Kennedy assassination look like a kid's game. The Freedom of Information Act is useless. We get a sex ed class in high school that explains how an erection works and then nothing. Until now. My information has been secreted out from behind the lines by actual married men, just like the microfilm in *The Dirty Dozen*.

This is the book they—your girlfriends, fiancées, or wives—don't want you to read. It tells the unvarnished truth from start to finish. This isn't necessarily how you feel about things, it's how I've seen them with my own eyes. As the Eagles once sang: "I could be wrong, but I'm not."

I promise only scant dubious advice, but here's some: Don't take any advice. John Gray, the author of the hugely successful *Men Are from Mars, Women Are from Venus*, is divorced a couple of times. His ex-wife is another one dishing out marital advice. Hypocrites.

I urge you to hide this book, that's how powerful it could be if it fell into the wrong hands. Simply take the cover off another book and hide this inside. Something innocuous or sports-themed would be good. She won't go looking in there.

PREPARING FOR THE INEVITABLE

"Bachelors know more about women than married men.
If they didn't they'd be married, too."
—H. L. MENCKEN

What are you going to do? You're going to get married, that's
what you're going to do. There is virtually no *if*, only *when*.
You have almost no choice except, possibly, where and with whom.
In the long run it's the best thing for you and, at the very least, the
alternatives are probably worse. Get married. Just do it.

It is as inevitable as the Super Bowl. You're going to have to
stop running around with every woman who consents to run
around with you. You're going to want the stability of a mature,
meaningful, and lasting relationship. You're going to want com-
panionship when you're old and withered. You're going to want
children, to start a family. These are natural feelings. It is entirely
natural to want these things. This is how society has carried on
for thousands of years, yet marriage is about as natural as Mount
Rushmore.

It is also natural to see all your friends get married and realize that somehow you are fast on your way to becoming an endan-
gered species, the last of a dying breed. You better get with the
program quickly or you are destined to become one of those

untouchable guys you hear about in India. You know, "he's over forty and never been married" means there must be something wrong with him. By extrapolation, you're either gay or afraid of commitment. You would be infinitely better off as a forty-something divorced guy; the rationale being that at least you're not afraid of commitment, albeit fleetingly.

Marriage is as unavoidable as taxes. You can avoid it, but at your peril. What else are you going to do? When was the last time you met a confirmed lifetime bachelor? Even you, you callous bastard, probably think there is something wrong with him. He's got all that freedom and he still doesn't look too happy—there must be something wrong with him. If he was a woman he would be called a spinster or an old maid. Even the idea of a man living his entire life without a wife seems strangely out of date, something from an Oscar Wilde drawing room comedy and, well, you know.

Marriage is all very well and good, but to a lot of single guys it seems like carrying love a little too far. H. L. Mencken said, "He mar-

ries best who puts it off until it is too late." When is the right time? Most of the men in our vast clinical survey said, "You will just know it." Of course, most of those same men were drinking heavily at the time, and were probably not the most reliable witnesses, but they were all sick and tired of having to try to polish up their own bullshit every time they met a new woman.

You may have noticed a creeping sense that "all the good ones are taken," that the available herd is thinning out and the new crop is too young for your aging spirit. You'd better act fast or there will soon be no women of quality left to marry. You're absolutely right.

Sometimes a man spends so much on his girlfriend he finally marries her for his money.

No matter how you get the urge to merge: loneliness, lust, resignation, desperation, a burning need to procreate, plain old-fashioned love, or because you want to be like everybody else—you're going to walk down that aisle looking like a lost little boy trying to find his mommy in a big department store. Like you're looking for an address. Or a life raft.

Even though your relationship must be pretty good for you to get to this place, I'm sure everyone you have ever met has told you that marriage is hard work. Of course marriage is a lot of work. Marriage must be pretty hard—half the time it doesn't work out and someone gets fired. Even the half that it does work out for, half the time it doesn't work. If you want your marriage to work get it a paper route . . . or read on.

Essentially marriage is getting two people together and throwing them into a Battle Royal cage for life—a fight to the death in which only one combatant emerges alive. If these two people from different backgrounds don't kill each other, if they somehow let love carry the day even in the heat of fierce arguments, despite everything else that happens—that's pretty good. That's a tough one. That's a fucking miracle.

I'm not suggesting that you shouldn't get married. For the record: The *Life Sentence* Institute strongly recommends getting married. Indeed, most of the men I spoke with said that they loved their wives and would do it all over again. (As opposed to most lawyers, who said that they would not do it—law school—all over again if given the choice. But then lawyers have the advantage of hindsight at $150 per hour.) They just wish they had been warned about some of the stuff that's in this book.

There is no way to prepare. You have your own past relationships to reflect upon, and while they have been instructive thus far, none of them have gone the distance, and at least one ended badly. So maybe you aren't the role model you're looking for.

You can look to your own parents, who, for about one-half of the population (those poor, undernourished children of divorce), are a clinic in what not to do. There is something to be said for that. You've seen what they did, now do the opposite. For the other half, those poor, overfed children of two-parent families, there will be something to be gleaned from their relationship, including, for many, what not to do.

TV, of course, is a ready source of information. A fount of dubious knowledge neatly packaged in thirty- and sixty-minute parables. You can tell instantly that these people are not real because none of them are in therapy where they so desperately belong. Being fictional precludes the need for TV characters to address the underlying issues confronting them. They don't harbor any anger from one episode to the next. Every episode is a variation on a central theme that begins roughly with "To the moon, Alice," and ends with "Baby, you're the greatest!"

Preparing for marriage is like preparing for death; you don't know what lies ahead and there's not much you can do about it. After you are pronounced "man and wife," the next time you are "pronounced" anything, it will be *dead*. Fortunately, this book offers little in the way of real advice, but here's some: Hope for the best, expect the worst. That way, when you're merely disappointed that things didn't work out as you dreamed they might, you'll be slightly relieved that things aren't as bad as you feared they could be. Then jump in the boat and row for your life.

Forsaking everything else, the good news is that you will always have a New Year's Eve date, and that is probably reason enough to go through with it.

COMPATIBILITY

"The only real argument for marriage is that it remains the best method for getting acquainted."

—HEYWOOD BROUN

know a couple who recently got divorced because they were incompatible. They didn't suffer from irreconcilable differences, they were just incompatible. They went out for over a year before they were married and it seems as though neither one of them ever thought to ask the other "what do you like to do?" (It is possible that he did ask, but he went into a trance when she answered, figuring, wrongly, that it was the same shit he liked to do.) Hard to believe, but they never noticed that they just didn't get along.

In his very funny book *High Fidelity*, Nick Hornby writes:

> *A while back when [we] agreed that what really matters is what you like, not what you are like, Barry proposed the idea of a questionnaire for prospective partners, a two- or three-page multiple-choice document that covered all the music/film/TV/book bases. It was intended to (a) dispense with awkward conversation, and (b) prevent a chap from leaping into bed with someone who might, at a later date, turn out to have every Julio Iglesias record ever made. It amused us at the time, although Barry ... went one stage further: he compiled*

the questionnaire and presented it to some poor woman he was interested in, and she hit him with it. But there was an important and essential truth contained in the idea, and the truth was that these things matter, and it's no good pretending that any relationship has a future if your record collections disagree violently, or if your favorite films wouldn't even speak to each other if they met at a party.

Of course you're not going to agree on everything; opposites do attract and you can cherish your differences. Republicans and Democrats can be compatible given proper supervision. In this great country of ours, people of different races, religions, and social backgrounds can learn to put aside these issues and find happiness together, learning and growing from the new awareness of each other's unique cultural sensibilities.

Still, I could never be with anyone who didn't appreciate Ella Fitzgerald, or had never seen *Casablanca.* Those are the very basic ground rules for compatibility with me. I'm not pushing for Tom Waits or *The Four Hundred Blows,* but if that's important to you, if that's part of who you are—even if it's Barry Manilow and *Die Hard*—you have a right to know that the woman you want to marry is With the Program. "Do you promise to be compatible" should be one of the wedding vows.

If you are not yet married, you really owe it to yourself to do this. Right now. Before it's too late. Get a piece of paper and a pen and draw up a list. Walk around the house. Flip through a few magazines. Write down questions about any topic that comes to mind. Is the toilet seat a major issue? What do you like to do on winter vacations? Do you play cards? Are you religious? What are your eating habits/neurotic dieting obsessions? Are you a morning person? A workaholic? A neat freak? A lazy slob? Do you read books? Where do you stand on abortion? How do you feel about televised sporting events? Do you have some vast unresolved dream of owning horses on a farm that we haven't discussed? Are you a closet drug addict? Do you hate my parents and friends? Are you gay? You don't want to find out that you have nothing in common with your wife on *The Newlywed Game*. And if anyone asks you where the strangest place you ever made whoopie is, the answer isn't "In da butt, Bob." Okay?

It's entirely possible that all this shit will never come up until you wake up one morning and find that you're married to a woman who isn't the woman you thought you married. Do you know about a book called *The Rules*? No? You should. Women read this book and pass it on, among themselves, like a joint. It contains the secrets to much of their seemingly bizarre behavior. The book advises women to be mysterious, not to give away too much. It says that if she has had a big problem or issue in her life, she should wait until the guy is already in love with her before she tells him about it. You find out about shit like this and it makes you want to not trust women.

I knew a guy in college who broke up with his beautiful, smart, cool girlfriend because she left the top off the toothpaste tube near the hairbrush. I'll grant you that this is an unpleasant, utterly avoidable, grody, marginally unhealthy thing, but—Get Over It, Mac. The same woman brushed her teeth with his dick at night and I didn't see him complaining about that. I'm sure the potential health consequences of that maneuver outweigh getting a hair in your toothpaste. His fastidious dedication to personal hygiene, it seems, was selective. In any case, it's not grounds for divorce. The guy was hitting over his average back then, and I'm pretty sure he's gay now, but the point remains: Get that shit out of the way before there are children to consider.

Make your peace with these personality quirks and shortcomings before it's too late. She doesn't cook? Send her to cooking school, order in, eat out, hire a cook, or get another wife. Don't get pissed off that you married a woman you know doesn't cook. Any of the above options are cheaper than a divorce, and these kinds of differences are indeed reconcilable if you plan ahead.

There are about a million things that you can name that will drive one person to madness about another person. Give most guys five minutes and they can find at least one potential defect in Claudia Schiffer. So, if you've got issues with a woman when you're going out with her, get it into the open, man. Fix it while you still have options, while you still have (what the late George Costanza called) "hand." Marriage

doesn't solve the problems you had when you were dating, it makes them permanent.

She has to do the same thing with you, only more so. It is incumbent upon you to stake a claim on your weaknesses and idiosyncrasies early on. Don't lay some heavy anal sex trip on her during the honeymoon. If that's what you're into, and there's nothing wrong with it, get security clearance before you order the wedding invitations. Whatever the thing is, map out and establish your territory. If you go nuts in traffic, that's your thing and you want to retain the right to go nuts in traffic for as long as you both shall live. If it's the hair in the toothpaste business, come out and let her know that that is where you draw the line in the sand. If she keeps it up, ditch her.

She was warned.

LIVING TOGETHER

"Every woman should marry—and no man."
—BENJAMIN DISRAELI

I f you've never lived with a woman before you get married, it stands to reason that there is a big adjustment ahead. But why is it still so hard if you've already been living together? Living together has nothing to do with compatibility, it is about adjusting to incompatibility. Wasn't the point of moving in together to get used to each other's rhythms, personal habits, and dysfunctional lifestyle? What about that?

In the old days of black-and-white movies, people (a) met, (b) fell in love, (c) kissed, (d) got married, (e) moved in together, (f) then had sex. Pretty much in that order. The reason they got married was so they could move in together and have sex. By the time they came out of the ether, they were already settled into the groove (or rut) they would inhabit for as long as they both shall live. But they had a lot less to compare against back in the good old days of the Hays Office.

Nowadays it goes something like (a) meet, (c) kiss, (f) have sex, (b) fall in love, (e) move in together, and (d) then get married. Everything's out of order. Now people move in together so they won't have to travel so far to have sex. You can see how there might be a problem bubbling up here.

It is clear that the whole idea behind people living together before they wed is to help avoid the pitfalls in modern relationships. By the time you've spent a year together in a one-bedroom apartment, you know each other's rhythms. You stop being so cloyingly polite. She talks on the phone to her girlfriends for hours at a time and you don't close the bathroom door, ever. You know the deal and make the necessary adjustments.

Still, it rarely seems to work out that way. Before the honeymoon is over both of your expectations change, and then the demons come out. Some weird alchemy overtakes normal people who have lived together in an essentially married lifestyle—it used to be called common law marriage—and they start from scratch once again. It is as though they went to an exclusive Eastern prep school but emerged from the experience uniquely unprepared for college.

You will learn something. Damon said that living with his wife before they got married allowed him to understand the real meaning of her hair. He came home to find Carrie screaming and crying, kicking her feet on the bed in utter despair. He braced himself for the worst; surely someone must have died to elicit this response. Not exactly. Carrie got a haircut she didn't like and was a teensy weensy bit upset about it. He didn't care. He loved her no matter what, with long hair or short. You see, as Damon explained, a man's identity is wrapped up in his job in the same way that a woman's identity is about her physical image. Ergo, a bad hair day is the equivalent of getting called on the carpet by your boss; a bad haircut is like getting fired; and a really bad haircut is like going bankrupt and being sent to jail. You would cry, too.

Living together is part of the "getting your ducks lined up in a row" thing. Living together prepares you for some of the things you can expect in a marriage. Sex becomes less important than it was. It's there. She's there. No hurry. Now or later, it's about the same. Taking a shower together is more about getting to work on time than some hot, soapy game.

Before you move in, you have to orchestrate sex. Who's sleeping at whose place? Change of clothes, toothbrush, shaving kit, etc. After you move in it's about orchestrating your life. You instantly cut your closet space in half and double your accountability. For example, living together makes it harder to see other women. She will probably know if you don't come home one night.

The deal with moving in together is that either you keep on living together or you don't. It's the same as a marriage, without the blood tests, the cake, and all the messy paperwork. You experience all the rhythms of being married and none of the responsibility. Which brings up the question: Why buy the cow when you get the milk for free? (Answer below.)

My friend Lambert has perfected the art form of getting the milk for free. He is on his fourth or fifth live-in girlfriend. Every time one moves out he has to replace some clothes, some kitchen gear, some CDs—but he always keeps the house, the car, and the dog. Of course, he has to replace the girl each time, too. The last one took the dog with her. "I loved that dog," he said.

(Answer: You buy the cow because she is threatening to leave the barn if you don't.)

BUYING THE RING

"A diamond is the hardest
substance known to man, especially
if he is trying to get it back."

Buying an engagement ring is, for most men, a terrifying experience. As well it should be. You've probably bought some jewelry for women in the past, specifically avoiding rings of any size or shape. One friend bought his girlfriend every piece of jewelry imaginable, beginning with a pair of earrings, followed by a bracelet and so on, until he'd seemingly exhausted all the possibilities. The girl was desperate for a ring, but he wanted to keep the commitment to a minimum and so he kept coming up with new items that were decidedly not rings. After the ankle bracelet he proffered a "slave" bracelet, and that was the end of his problem because she left and he started the cycle over again with the next girl.

Many women believe the chief foundation for true love is a large stone. This is further proof that size does matter. If love is something which can be measured in carats, a big ring makes an awfully compelling argument. The Diamond Council suggests that an engagement ring should cost about three months' salary. I'm sure the Egg Council would like their product to cost at least an hour's wage, but nobody ever listens to them.

Buying a ring is enormously expensive, perhaps more expensive than anything you ever bought for yourself, except your car—but that was different. The ring is a token of your everlasting love for your betrothed and a measure of your worth as a human being and a provider. Whether you step up to the plate or not, everybody's going to know. You're making a statement. The ring says "How'm I doin'?" for both of you. Go large, as big as you can. Think "ostentatious." Think "wow!" Think "skating rink." Buying a ring should hurt a little bit, but you will be far better off poor-but-happy than wealthy-but-miserable.

There are basically two ways to do this ring thing. You can research the deal on your own and take your chances, or you can get her involved. With Plan A, the more traditional approach, you have the element of surprise working for you. Even if you have discussed getting married with your girlfriend, actually asking is a well-orchestrated sneak attack. (Be very careful if you talk about getting married in conceptual terms. This is not idle chatter and can work against you. A seemingly innocent statement about your future like "I think I'll want to have children someday" opens you up to a lot of conversational tangents you might not have considered. Trying to stop the cross-examination can be like trying to stuff a mattress into a suitcase.) The D-Day invasion is a good model of both stealth and execution. Your pending engagement should receive top secret status, especially in the unlikely event that she says no.

Plan B means getting her involved and thus removes some of the surprise for both of you, except for the actual moment, location, and method of the popping of the question itself. Which, by the way, will be the last moment you're even nominally in charge of things in your relationship, so savor this moment. You may have been calling the shots up till then, but the sound of the popping of the question is the Maginot Line in every relationship. That's when she says yes or no. Either way, she is establishing a pattern that you can ask questions and she then tells you what's up—and her decision is final. After that you start planning the wedding, which is her showcase. Then you have the honeymoon, and then the honeymoon is over, as we shall see.

Buying a ring means getting an intense crash course in a subject most men avoid—Diamonds. You're like a CIA operative getting briefed for a deep-cover assignment behind enemy lines. You are going to know all about some things called "cut," "clarity," and "carat." You will become a certified expert on the subject of the "three Cs," and a whole bunch of different shapes and settings, exactly at the moment your tutor, the jeweler, swipes your credit card.

Get to know your jeweler. Diamonds are a boy's best friend. There is almost no hole so deep you can't dig your way out of it with diamonds. Besides, a diamond carries with it an implicit bonus (see "Blow Jobs") for good behavior. This is not the last piece of jewelry you're going to buy and you might as well be friends with the guy you're giving all your money to. Think of him as your junior partner in the business that is your wife.

POPPING THE QUESTION

"Love consists in overestimating the difference
between one woman and another."
—GEORGE BERNARD SHAW

Nothing can prepare you for popping the question. Nothing.
No amount of rehearsal is going to make this task any easier.
Think of the biggest question you've ever asked anyone in your
entire life and it seems like a pebble compared to this mountain. All
the other questions you will ever ask feel like "Could you pass the
salt?" when put alongside "Will you marry me?" In fact, think about
the biggest question anyone has ever asked anyone else in real
life—or even in the movies—and almost all of them will pale in
comparison. Maybe "To be or not to be?" stands up, but "Will you
marry me?" is gigantically huge.

You may want to narrow the odds before you make an ass of
yourself and ask a woman to marry you only to have her say no. A
lot of guys want to nose around the issue, cautiously checking their
standing, not confirming, not denying. Sharon was a hotshot execu-
tive with million-dollar decision-making green-light power, but she
was living with Ted in a house they bought together, waiting, as she
put it, "for some guy to ask her a question." Eventually he did, she
did, they did, and a year later they got divorced. But that's beside
the point. The point is that Ted successfully shortened the odds by

moving in with her and then buying a house with her. They were moving in a positive direction, and he had the "mo" on his side. What was she going to say? No? You take the living room, I get the kitchen.

Here's the same deal in reverse. After Jake moved in, Andrea gave him a deadline: "I want a ring on my finger by August 31 or you move out." She was not going to "throw away the best years of my life on some guy" who was basically a freeloader. Put up or shut up. It was a little tense around their place as the clock was ticking down to zero. Every time they went out to dinner she was expecting a surprise. He seriously considered waiting until she packed up the last of his things before bringing out the little black box, but he beat the deadline by two weeks. She played hardball and it worked. He took the bait and they all lived happily ever after.

Where and how you pop the question says a lot about you and how you see your relationship. If you ask in the middle of a ski run, it shows that you are impulsive and wanted to make sure that she could ski black diamonds before you got in too deep.

If you saw *Moonstruck* you know that the proper way to propose is on bended knee in a restaurant full of people. (She— Cher—said yes both times.)

One guy hid the ring in a plate of strawberries after dinner, which he practically had to force his girlfriend to eat. I see a lot of surprise birthday parties in their future.

If you ask her to marry you after sex, it's like offering her a promotion for a job well done. But, of course, you will be having sex again very soon.

If you try a more casual approach, simply saying "Let's get married," you may hear a buzzer, followed by Alex Trebek asking you to rephrase it in the form of a question ("What is 'Let's get married'?"). It conveys a lot of the same sentiment, but it's still nice to ask.

My parents got engaged after three dates but, of course, they were rabidly horny. Imagine trying that move nowadays; no matter how in love you were (or thought you were), she'd slap a restraining order on your ass before the fourth date.

One very realistic guy asked his girlfriend, "Will you make me miserable for the rest of my life?" And she said yes! (Alas, they never made it to the altar.)

No matter how you plan your sales pitch, that ring is going to feel like an atom bomb in your pocket. The way your palms will be sweating will be like getting stoned around your parents or having a boner on the beach, you'll be sure that everyone is on to you. They must be.

THE BACHELOR PARTY

"Love is one long sweet dream and
marriage is the alarm clock."

The miracle of a bachelor party is that it exists at all. It is a testament to the bottomless gullibility of women that they allow this shameless bastion of male hedonism to continue. I occasionally hear about a bride-to-be who says that as long as the groom-to-be doesn't actually fuck the hooker or doesn't catch a disease, it's okay. No one believes her, but at least she let her future husband go to a hotel room with a team of female mud wrestlers. Of course, no one has ever told the truth about what actually happens at one of these stag rituals. Whether it turns out to be wet and wild or just harmless voyeuristic fun, the fraternal understanding demands that you never tell. Never—as in not ever. You agree on a story before you leave the room and stick with it to the grave. This is not a lie. It is part of the code. *Omerta.*

A bachelor party is a safe haven, like driving recklessly in a car with diplomatic license plates—you're untouchable for one night. This is why the bachelor party is so important. If you've always wanted to try something—two girls, a midget, a giantess, whatever—do it. Get it out of your system. After that night you will spend the rest of your life resisting temptation at every turn; yield to it now. These girls will make you think you're as good as you think you are.

In truth, bachelor parties are really for the married guys. They don't get out much with live nude girls and they get so excited by the possibilities.

Guys always come back from a bachelor party wondering: Why can't my girlfriend/wife be more like those girls? Why doesn't she carry a can of Reddi Whip in her purse? Or get into simulated lesbian scenes with her cute girlfriends so I can watch? Why doesn't she dance topless in the living room and shake her tits in my face? Don't try this at home, cowboy.

If you get into the position where your friends have arranged for a hooker—a real one, not some dancer you try to cut a deal with once she gets there—and you go into the bedroom with her: Do you do it? This is a tough decision. You haven't forsaken all others yet—and it is a big "yet." This will almost certainly be your last chance to score without violating a Commandment and, in your defense, it's not like you consciously went out and seduced someone. It's almost like taking a hit off a joint at a concert, it was *there*.

On the flip side, if you go into the bedroom and don't do it, what do you tell your friends? If you admit it, does that just make you look like a big fucking pussy who wasted their money and the chick's time? (She doesn't care—the meter is running—but your friends might like a shot at her before they get too drunk.)

If you've had sex with a lot of women in your life, what difference will one more make?

YOUR WILD OATS

"A married man is a bachelor
whose luck has run out."

Make sure that you've sowed all your oats—wild or otherwise—before you get married. This advice comes from a
guy who once dated my sister, then married someone I slept with.
Who would know better?

You are never, ever going to stop ogling, admiring, and desiring
women. Other women. Never. You'll stop jacking off first. (As if.)
But you had better have fucked in every position, in every place,
with every nationality in the United Nations—every color, size, and
shape of woman—before you say "I do," or you will never be happy,
given that you are about to surrender your privileges to do so with
any of those people ever again.

If you haven't sown ("sown" and "sowed" are interchangeable;
look it up) your wild oats, you really have no right popping the
question. Do your fucking around *first*. And don't fuck around after
you're engaged. If, on the off chance you get caught before the wedding, your life is going to get much, much worse. Quickly. In an age
where you normally would have to commit a $100 million fuck-up
or a particularly heinous crime to be publicly censured, this is the
fast track. If the invitations have already gone out you can be

absolutely certain that everyone you ever met will know exactly what a lowlife you are. The deeply hurt, ex-future Mrs. You and her vast, vengeful PR staff will see to that. The next several weeks will be a living hell, as you make a halfhearted attempt at selling a cock-and-bull story to your friends and relatives about how "it just didn't work out." People will whisper about you—"isn't that the guy who . . . ?" You will be branded for life.

If you knew in advance which woman you were going to marry, I am certain that you would make your penultimate girlfriend the guinea pig for every sexual experiment you ever heard about. You would comb back issues of *Penthouse Forum* for kinky new ideas. She would be a nasty girl, a super freak, the kind you don't take home to mother. Kenny says: "Unfortunately, you just don't know when you're going to meet the right girl, so don't take any chances; abuse all of them."

Did you know there are people who still are virgins when they get married? These unfortunate souls stand a good chance of freaking out once they find out what they've been missing all along. That's their problem, but the above advice still holds. You either have no wild oats to sow, or are content in choosing not to sow them. In either case, be prepared to live with the consequences. You had your chance.

THE BRIDAL SHOWER

> "Marriage is a partnership
> where no matter how good a husband is,
> his wife is still the better half."

The bridal shower is a good thing. Her girlfriends are going to get together for a party in which they give her lingerie, kitchen stuff, and sex toys. Nothing wrong with that, as long as you don't have to be there. You really, really don't want to go to this shindig. And the bigger it is, the more you don't want to be there.

In our increasingly genderless society, it is becoming more common to have a couples wedding shower, known in the trade as a "Jack and Jill shower." Fuck that. Play golf. Watch football. Cleaning the garage is a better way to kill a weekend afternoon. Anything is. More to the point, you might get roped into this as part of the wedding package, but you have no right to inflict this distaff bullshit on your friends. They will resent you for it, as you would if they did it to you. By the way, you will only see other married guys at these affairs. Single Guy is out there where the grass is greener, doing the anything else that you would rather be doing. (He's laughing at you.)

Here's what happens after the low-fat, low-flavor luncheon. The women form a circle like a coven of witches. The bride-to-be reads each card, unwraps each box, and parades each gift around for the others to ooh and ahh over like an incantation. They do this with every gift, in turn, so no one feels cheated that their gift was prejudicially left unopened. (Women can be incredibly competitive about junk like this because they don't fully understand baseball.) If you get roped into this travesty of femininity, by gift number 3 the concept will get a little threadbare ("How 'bout if we just do this later after everyone leaves?"); by number 5 your toe is tapping by itself and your phony smile is beginning to droop; at number 8 you stifle a yawn; by number 10 you yawn openly and don't give a damn who sees it. More than a dozen and you will say "Fuck this shit," and excuse yourself to go take a nap.

The good thing about the bridal shower is that she will get some lingerie that you didn't have to buy. I'm always self-conscious buying lingerie, trying to estimate her curves and measurements with my hands. "She's about this big," I say, miming holding two grapefruits in midair while consciously trying not to mentally undress the entire store. Lingerie is great when you're single, but it's almost totally wasted on married women. They're on to the lingerie scam. When I was eleven years old, my sister and I got my parents a Foosball game for their anniversary. Same thing with lingerie. You are really getting her a present that you want to play with. What does she want or need it for? You already bought into her seduction act, now there's nothing you can do about it.

Sure it adds a little sex and spice to the routine when she puts on the old uniform—it's a little nostalgic, like Old Timers' Day out at the ballpark—but if she's wearing skimpy little nothings after the first year of your marriage, there's a good chance she wants something from you and, ironically, perhaps, you gave her the tools to come and get it.

If you want to see women in lingerie, go to a strip club. Then, when you are worked up into a frenzy of sexual lust and desire, come home and ravage your wife like God intended.

PLANNING THE WEDDING

"Men differ from Women.
You never see young men sitting around
talking about their dream weddings."

—CHARLES COSART

Being engaged is a weird gray area. You're not married, but neither are you exactly single. You're neither here nor there, like being on an airplane. It's the romantic equivalent of being in cyberspace. You made promises but they have no legal standing. The engagement ring is like signing a lease with an option to buy. A down payment.

Okay, you've paid a fortune for a diamond engagement ring. You've mustered the courage to ask the woman you love to marry you and be your wife. She said yes. You picked a date. Now what do you do?

Get the hell out of the way, that's what you do! Get a ringside seat and watch ver-ry carefully. Preparing for a wedding will be like getting a postgraduate degree in Your Wife-to-Be. You'll see your little woman morph into an emotional medicine ball, nearly simulating pregnancy. You'll get to watch her mother, your mother-in-law-to-be, in action. Pay close attention. No matter how much everyone denies it, no matter how much you hope and pray it can't possibly be true, you are getting a crystal ball preview of the future. You're in a *Twilight Zone* episode of your own future, thirty years ahead.

You want to pay attention, not because you can change any of this from happening in the future, but because you don't want to be caught by surprise when it does come to pass.

You must know, before the whole shooting match gets under way, that this is her show. The wedding is about your Bride. As proof, there are dozens of magazines for brides but none for grooms. All the advice you're likely to get about your own wedding could be printed on the back side of a business card from the tux rental place, echoing Spencer Tracy's immortal advice about acting: "Just know your lines and don't bump into the furniture."

Your wife has dreamed of this day all her life. While you and G.I. Joe were out on the killing fields after school, she was in her Betty Crocker dream house imagining you coming home from a hard day at the office. She has been waiting for you, and is poised now like a cobra, ready to strike. There is an old adage that states: Marriage is a condition most women aspire to and most men submit to. You have feared this day, and not without good reason.

At least her father is paying for it.

A short list of wedding things about which you will be consulted, but which your considered opinion will not carry much weight: the size of the guest list, the guests, the bridal registry, the videotape, the band, the music, the menu, the cake, the color scheme, the flowers, where to register, the patterns, the photographer, the invitations, the number of bridesmaids and corresponding groomsmen. The wedding is the first real test of the marriage. There are a million details to consider and you should at least pretend to give a shit about the color of the wedding invitation, not that it matters. In reality, the best man is your only call.

Sandra Tsing Loh wrote about her wedding plans: "As the . . .

bride plans her Special Day, the groom becomes an extraneous character, a rubber mascot head, a blank screen upon which the ensuing drama of the bridal breakdown is to be shakily projected." This is pretty much a show-up job for you, and yet you ultimately shoulder most or all of the blame for anything that could possibly go wrong. Now you're beginning to get the message. The only song about grooms is "Get Me to the Church on Time."

If your sainted mother-in-law-to-be is going to be involved in planning the affair, I guarantee she is going to go overbudget, whatever the budget is. There is no budget she cannot exceed. She's like some kind of Olympic high jumper going for the gold, you raise the bar and she'll clear it. She will ask you questions or ask for your opinion only when she already has decided the answer. Once she has made up her mind, she might test you just to see what you're made of. (Just like your mother.) She'll fuck with your head, and there's not a goddamn thing you can do about it. Weigh your answers carefully, son, this is not a rational person you're dealing with.

Some men frown on big weddings, and well they should. This fairy-tale stuff is not the kind of thing upon which you can build a successful, lasting relationship. It is wholly unrealistic, leading to grossly exaggerated expectations, after which anything would be a letdown. Keep this in mind as you turn around to face the assembled guests for the first time as Husband and Wife, walking back up the aisle to a thunderous ovation. Unless you're an entertainer, ballplayer, or politician, this may well be the last standing "O" you are ever going to get. Enjoy it if you're not in shock. It goes straight downhill from this moment forward.

The upside of a big wedding is that you'll get a lot of gifts. Sadly, you couldn't give a rat's ass about most of these things. You're not likely to get a Jet Ski or any cool stereo stuff, and almost no one ever gives power tools (even though a belt sander would probably get a lot more use than a gravy boat). If you have a hard time getting excited about a fish server, think about it this way: If some sucker didn't buy it for you, sooner or later you'd have to do it yourself. Isn't that $200 cake knife looking a whole lot sexier now? The downside is that you have to write thank-you notes for every gift. Well, somebody has to do it. You also have to remember what people got you so you can whip out their gift when they come over to your house. They want and expect to see that fish server in action.

When making the invitation list, think seriously about the kind of gift you might expect from that person. You laugh at this notion now, but when push comes to shove, you will weigh your friendships in gold, or porcelain.

THE MAIN EVENT

"I was married by a judge.
I should have asked for a jury."
—GEORGE BURNS

The wedding itself is a joyous and wonderful celebration of love and life. It marks the most dramatic transition in your life, with legal, religious, social, and moral implications. It is also probably the greatest day of her life.

You, on the other hand, will stare down the aisle like you were going skydiving for the first time, looking out the door of the plane. Your adrenaline will be pumping and you'll feel like the bravest, craziest motherfucker in town, but the married guys will all look at you like you were taking a puff of your first cigarette. You're going to try to look cool, but you will be more than just a tad nervous about the whole thing, as well you should be. This is a big step, nay, a giant leap, and no one can help you now. You are the most "on your own" you have ever been, or ever will be. Stark naked. You're signing over half of everything you will ever have in your life to some chick you met at a party less than two years ago. She's the lollipop in white coming down the runway straight at you like a heat-seeking missile.

You will go through a whole gamut of emotions, mostly a profound sense of relief that it's over, like final exams. Finally people will stop nudging you about when are you going to get married, and details of the wedding. Now they'll start to ask you when you're planning to have children.

Still photographs are okay, a part of the package, but you must insist—absolutely—that the wedding not be videotaped. First of all, getting married is a really nerve-racking experience. You get one or two rehearsals, then it's showtime. Saying your wedding vows in front of God (and his really intimidating robed servant), your family and friends in some fancy, unfamiliar place is tough enough, but now there's a total stranger shining a bright light in your face, capturing your awkwardness on video for posterity. Unless you are among the one percent of the population who work in front of the camera, you probably don't know how upsetting it can be. There is no way you will look good. As you fumble for the ring you can imagine your progeny in years to come saying, "Look what a dork Dad was."

The resulting video only makes for worthwhile viewing long after the fact, when people who were at the wedding are dead ("Oh look, it's Uncle Icky, he died"). Then, after the divorce, you can play it on rewind and see yourself walking back up the aisle, a single man again. It's like the joke about what happens when you play a country-and-western song backwards—the guy sobers up, gets out of jail, gets his girl back, gets his job back, gets his truck back, and gets his dog back.

Just for a laugh, suggest that they replace the wedding march with the *Mission: Impossible* theme song.

By the way, what ever happened to "obey" in the list of things the wife was going to do in the marriage vows? "Obey" has been deleted in a tidal wave of postmodern feminism, and there does not seem to have been a memo, a fax, an e-mail, nothing to let the unsuspecting bridegroom population know that they are not going to be obeyed. The world is going to hell in a handbasket because one word got zapped from the vows and no one was told until it was too late to do anything about it. Have, hold, love, honor, and cherish are all nice thoughts, they're all good for her, but what's in it for you? Not a damn thing. Not much anyway. "Honor" is pretty nebulous terminology when compared to "obey," which is written in stone. No ifs, ands, or buts with "obey"; "honor" is a judgment call. Even when "obey" was in the lineup, it was really only an ace in the hole. The bride still held the winning hand most of the time, but when the other vows failed, at least you could fall back on "obey."

THE WEDDING NIGHT

"Never impress a woman,
because if you do she'll expect you to
keep up to the standard for
the rest of your life."

—W. C. FIELDS

The wedding night has lost some of its luster over the past few decades. It is not the "Big Night" event it used to be, as you have probably been sleeping with the blushing bride for months, maybe years, by this time. There is not much chance her mother is going to give your bride an instructional chat about what to expect in the course of performing her wifely duties. She could probably teach Mom a thing or two.

Even so, you will feel different. Undoubtedly you're going to say something like "Hello wife" or "Hello, Mrs. Smith." (Of course, it's always better if you use your own name in this instance.) You  are an idiot if you don't, because you won't have another wedding night opportunity again (for a while, at least), and you want to get into the habit of calling her "wife" as soon as possible. You can't keep calling her your "babe" after you're married. Save that moniker for your girlfriend after your wife leaves you.

Still, spending a night in a hotel in your hometown is fun. Room service, cable movies, plenty of clean towels and you don't have to clean up. These are all good things.

For many men, their wedding night is their first time with a married woman, and first times are harder to come by as you get older.

THE HONEYMOON

"No matter who you marry, you wake up
married to someone else."

—DAMON RUNYON

I was an usher at the wedding of a boyhood friend named Mitchell. Shortly after he and his wife, Jackie, returned from their two-and-a-half-week honeymoon in Hawaii I called him. "How's married life treating you?" I asked.

"It's a lot of work," he answered.

A LOT OF WORK? The guy had been in Hawaii. On his honeymoon. Playing golf, ferchrissakes! What part of that is a lot of work? Chipping out of a sand trap? Putting downhill? Driving the cart?

I can only surmise that it isn't easy spending seventeen consecutive days and nights with any one other living creature (more or less alone on a desert island), no matter how in love you are. You have already run out of your "A" material by the third date. You have survived the past several months with all the tumult of the wedding, which followed quickly on the heels of the engagement and the planning thereof. Now that shit is behind you. The wedding and party only took about eight hours, if that, so the retelling of it, the postmortem, should last about 192 hours: twenty-four virtual hours recounting each real one experienced. So after eight days together, you don't have anything left to talk about and you've still got the better part of a week to kill.

As Hugh Grant's character describes it in a telling scene from the film *Four Weddings and a Funeral,* "Marriage is just a way of getting out of an embarrassing pause in conversation."

Clearly, Mitchell had not seen the movie.

A honeymoon is like Christmas vacation after final exams. It is a continuation of the myth you try to create at the wedding. It's totally unreal. I have yet to find the man who says that marriage is a vacation. There should be a honeymoon for every major event in your life. If you start a new job, move, or buy a new car, you should take two weeks off immediately.

You simply must enjoy your honeymoon for the simple reason that when it's over, the honeymoon is over.

REALITY SETS IN

"Marriage is the way a man finds out what kind of husband his wife would have preferred."

—ANON.

Marriage is like losing your shore leave privileges, permanently. She is always there. You can depend on her to be there. That's good and that's bad. She is like the bounty hunters in *Butch Cassidy and the Sundance Kid.* They never go away. Butch finally turns to the Kid and says, "Who are those guys?" Well, those guys are your wife. It's like having Scottie Pippen defending you—everywhere you turn, she's there. You can't fake her out, and she's got Lo-Jack on your ass in case you get lost or stolen. For no particular reason she wants to know where you are at all times, and it behooves you to go along.

The really good news is that she has an enormous capacity to put up with you and all your shit. Think about it. You probably wouldn't. And even then you sometimes wonder how you live with yourself. In *Tootsie*, Dustin Hoffman comes to the realization that "Men are shits. It hit me when I realized that I wouldn't take myself out or go to bed with me."

Still, she will want to remake you. Remember the song "Marry the Man Today" from *Guys and Dolls*? She actually thinks that you will change. Who are we kidding here? You won't change. Men are consistent, reliable, dependable creatures. Natalie Wood once said: "The only time a woman really succeeds in changing a man is when he's a baby." Men don't change. You can count on men not changing. They stay the same at an alarmingly increasing rate. Men take pride in becoming old dogs who can't be taught new tricks. Men become caricatures of themselves, exaggerated versions of themselves. The only thing worse than a woman marrying a man to reform him is a man who marries a woman to educate her.

After you're married, the rules change in subtle ways. You can't take anything for granted. I asked my friend Murray if he wanted to go skiing in Utah. His wife keeps him on a pretty short leash so he said that I would have to ask her for permission for him to go skiing. He reasoned that she has a lot of practice saying no to him, but she was on unfamiliar turf with me. In the ensuing confusion he escaped for the weekend with her blessing. Before we left she called to thank me for her trip to Florida, explaining that there was always a quid pro quo. It was an auction and I basically just started the negotiation with a fat opening bid: "Three days in Utah to the gentleman, do I hear four days in South Beach? Yes! Four days in South Beach to the lady, going once . . ." And this is how things get done. It is a simple poker game. I'll see your bet and raise you. This is how we choose to think of it, because the idea that we've signed up for a lifetime extortion shakedown is too much to bear.

Fred says that the way to have a happy, lasting marriage is to travel constantly. Road trips give you a sense of longing, freshness— I haven't seen you in a while, you're pretty good looking, let's get it on. If you don't run around on her, you'll both be horny. Bonus reunion sex. If you don't travel on business, separate vacations are a good idea. You will come back to each other with a whole bunch of new stuff to talk about. David and Gail were so stressed out before their wedding that they were actually considering separate honeymoons. Rodney Dangerfield's advice is, "We sleep in separate rooms, we have dinner apart, we take separate vacations—we're doing everything we can to keep our marriage together."

Your wife will talk your ear off. Perhaps she kept this little trick a secret before you inked the contract, or perhaps you simply didn't notice while the game was still afoot. Either way, there is something about returning from a honeymoon that sets the conversational endorphins loose in a woman.

The old bromide says that marriage is an endless conversation in which the more the woman talks, the less the man listens. Johnny says the essence of marriage is that you are going to find out about more bullshit you couldn't care less about, and you will have to pay attention and know this stuff backwards and forwards, because there will be any number of pop quizzes on this material, like oral exams in grad school. It will sound like the adults on the old *Peanuts* TV specials, "Wah wah wah wah wah." Just utter gibberish.

One well-intentioned book in the secret women's part of the store, called *Men: A Translation for Women,* by Joan Shapiro, M.D. (another know-it-all "Doctor"), has a chapter about "What he's thinking about when he's tuning you out." She says that for men, talking "demands a kind of continuous involvement . . . too much connection and emotion . . . for constant responses." Maybe she's right. Maybe we men just tune out because it's too emotionally demanding to be connected all the time. Dr. Shapiro didn't consider the possibility that we tune out because it's mostly the same old bullshit and we've heard it before. After a while you've both heard it all before.

MEET YOUR WIFE

"A man is incomplete until he is married.
Then he is finished."
—ZSA ZSA GABOR

You did not marry your wife. You married your bride, who used to be your fiancée, who used to be your girlfriend, who used to be a chick. That chick was very much like your wife in appearance, and in other ways. As your fiancée, she was your wife without portfolio. Ludwig Borne, whoever the hell he was, said: "A sweetheart is milk, a bride is butter, and a wife is cheese." He was no dairy farmer, but he nailed this one on the head. You are both transformed by the wedding. She was just "(do you take) this woman" in the morning, and by night she was "your lawful wedded wife." She is reborn, a new person altogether, with a new name and a new agenda.

Part of her portfolio is her controlling interest in you and what used to be your life, singular. Now, as a result of the merger, it is your life, plural. You may have been the controlling force, the guiding light when you were a single couple, but that was then and this is forever. This is now and she will set the tone, the social calendar, the budget. You become like the Queen of England, the figurehead in a constitutional monarchy. Your home is your castle, but your broadly perceived powers cover up a lack of real authority.

Your wife will spend much more time thinking about your relationship than you do. She'll think about it when you're sleeping, when you're awake, if you've been bad or good, she's all over it, for goodness sake. She is a nonstop relationship-assessing machine. Every tone of voice is measured by a panel of ultrasensitive instruments embedded in her skin. If she says "What's the matter?" there is an extremely good chance that something is the matter. The great Catskills comic Mal Z. Lawrence says that when married guys wake up, they look at their wives first thing in the morning, and say: "Have I done anything you don't like yet? How about we just shake hands and call it a day?"

No matter how long you knew her before you were married, whether you lived together or not, you will never fully understand this person. You may have grown up with a houseful of sisters, consider yourself a feminist, whatever—but you will spend a good deal of time scratching your head. The reasons for this stem from the fact that men and women are different—in case you hadn't noticed. (Good thing you bought the book, huh Einstein?) Being a woman means that she is mysterious, bordering on devious. She has an alarming capacity to surprise you. Jerry and Dana have been together since high school, more than twenty years, and he admits that she can still throw him a knuckleball. This need not be the case.

If you want some insight into your wife you should read *Cosmo*. (When she's not looking, of course.) They're telling you, in very explicit detail, what's going on in their shrewd little minds, what they want and how they aim to get it. This could be the most important thing you will ever read and you would never, ever pick it up on your own. There is no hint of the insidious material that lies beneath the sexy Scavullo cover. Reading women's magazines is like finding the cipher that decodes all the enemy's transmissions in wartime, the key to all the apparent mysteries of female behavior. We're being invited into the opposing team's locker room, and this is their playbook.

In contrast, men's magazines tell us nothing. Jerry Seinfeld says, "There's very little advice in men's magazines, because men don't think there's a lot they don't know. Women do. Women want to learn. Men think, 'I know what I'm doing, just show me somebody naked.'" Our magazines tell us what we want to hear or already think we know about ourselves, by people just like us—what could we possibly know about it? It's all idle conjecture. No husband can ever know as much about himself as his wife thinks she knows about him.

It's good to have a wife for business and social purposes. She is a sign of your success. Mixing metaphors, who you marry says more about you than the clothes that make you or the food that you are. You get invited out together. Everyone expects her, and you don't have to spend half the night introducing her. You get mentioned as a group. You are thought of as a unit. Single guys get a plus-one sometimes. Your girlfriend was only known as "and Guest."

Here's a good rule to follow: When in doubt, put your wife on a pedestal. You don't even notice her pimples. If you do, don't acknowledge them, don't flinch. Steel your nerves. She's testing your resolve. The *Life Sentence* Institute strongly recommends overlooking these blemishes, complimenting her any time it comes to mind, and praising her myriad virtues in a loud, clear voice as often as possible, especially if she's already heard it before. Without rules like this, there would be anarchy.

FIGHTING WITH YOUR WIFE

"The best part about married life is the fights.
The rest is merely so-so."
—THORNTON WILDER

"If it weren't for marriage, men and women would
have to fight with total strangers."
—ANON.

I love boxing. They get these two guys in the ring, each there with the sole intention of beating the other guy up. They have trained long and hard for this moment, but before they can start pounding on one another, the referee gives them some very civilized instructions: "I want a clean fight, no low blows. Always keep your guard up. Break when I tell you to break. In case of a knockdown, go to a neutral corner. Come out fighting at the bell." There should be a little disclaimer at the wedding like this after you say "I do" and before you kiss the bride.

When you were single and had a fight with your girlfriend, you had options. You could call a cab to drive you off from a bad date and out of that relationship. You could make one phone call and the whole problem would be resolved—the chick wouldn't be bothering you anymore. You could drop a box full of her shit off at the apartment and she would be gone, gone, gone, like a big train from

Memphis. Poof! Pull up her number in your electronic organizer and hit delete, it's like she never existed.

That ain't gonna happen here. Your options aren't looking too good, my friend. Nothing you fought about before is going to be close to what you get into after you get married. The stakes are higher. Prenuptial arguments are like the tryouts in Bridgeport before taking the show to Broadway.

Since fights with your wife are inevitable, remember that she's still a chick, which means that she's always just moments away from imploding under the weight of her own neuroses. You are more or less responsible for seeing that this does not happen. Put differently, women can be a little emotional at times. You love each other, which may prove to be helpful, but she can (and occasionally will) turn on you, like a dog. Always side with the hysterical woman, then back out the door.

Don't take yourself too seriously. You might have a preponderance of evidence on your side. Your closing argument was brilliant. The jury is leaning in your favor. But, according to Rob Becker's brilliant one-man show *Defending the Caveman,* "Women are not hindered by logic." Which raises the question: What are you fighting for? What are you going to win? Consider the long-term, worst-possible-case scenario of winning a hotly contested argument with your wife: She manages to misconstrue everything you said in the heat of battle so that all she heard in the course of an hour is that you think she's stupid and you don't love her anymore, and then you spend the rest of your life apologizing and trying to get out of the doghouse . . . for what? Is a Pyrrhic victory worth winning? If you assume the worst-case scenario, you'll be pleasantly surprised when merely most of it comes true.

Go for the win, but not the kill. Your wife doesn't work for you, and she's not getting paid to take your shit. If you bring out the heavy artillery, she will use it against you later, until you can no longer identify what you were fighting about in the first place. You may want to break out of the clinch and make sure you're on the same page. And whatever you do, don't let her start to cry, because then you made her cry, and as soon as she starts the waterworks, you just lost on a TKO. Ease up on the throttle if you sense there are tears a-comin'. Winning isn't everything, and if she's pissed at you it's going to be hard for anybody else to be happy.

Choose your words carefully. No matter how hot things get, never, EVER use the c-word. It is like a live wire inserted directly into her cerebral cortex. "Bitch" is okay under certain circumstances. Even "Fucking idiot" can be justifiable when she is acting like a fucking idiot. "Piece of shit" is a low blow, a little too graphic for my taste, but essentially no problem. (Note: "Motherfucker" and "Sonofabitch" are technically incorrect in her case. "Cocksucker" is irrelevant, and may be greeted with "You wish," or words to that effect.) Whenever she says "What do you mean?" there is a very good chance that she knows exactly what you mean. She's on to you. Say what you mean and mean what you say because you will have to live with what you say and do in the heat of battle. Muhammad Ali, the Greatest, said that his toughest fight was with his first wife. What chance do you have?

Get over it—quickly. It doesn't matter if you win, lose, or draw ... move on. Don't gloat if you win, take your lumps like a man when you lose, and most importantly don't take it personally no matter what. You probably are or have been or will be all the things she calls you. Fights with your wife are like pulses on a heart chart, blips on a radar screen. *Ping!* They'll happen every day. *Ping!* By the time all is said and done, you'll have more tiffs, spats, squabbles, disagreements, arguments, screaming matches with your wife than everyone else in the world combined. *Ping!* Win a round, lose a round . . . it makes no difference. It was only one in a scheduled ten-thousand-round bout that nobody wins. It's going to be a long fight, a fight to the death, so don't get too caught up in any one particular skirmish. You have no time to savor a victory before the next battle gets under way.

Try the Bob and Emily Hartley route: Agree to never go to bed angry. It is true that they were, in fact, actually fictional characters in a television show, portrayed by actors who were mouthing words scripted for them by a team of highly paid comedy writers who could get out of any problem in twenty-four minutes. You want to be careful about using TV characters as role models. Still, it's a beautiful notion, and one that is almost humanly impossible to achieve because, if you stay married for a mere twenty-five years, that's over nine thousand daily opportunities for each of you to go to bed angry, times two. Have you ever heard of anything or anyone going 18,000 and 0? Even Joe DiMaggio's streak came to an end, and he only hit safely in fifty-six consecutive games. And he only did it once in his career. (Further, it is well documented that he and Marilyn Monroe went to bed angry a lot.)

Lose graciously . . . and often. Fighting leads inexorably to talking about your feelings, so don't start what you can't finish. Gary's father said that "the secret to a long, happy marriage is learning to admit when you're wrong . . . when you're right." Failing that, send her flowers the next day with a note that says "You're sorry," and live to fight another day.

"A husband is a man who has lost his liberty
in the pursuit of happiness."

Man evolved not—as some so-called scientists would have you believe—from apes, but from dogs. It is in our nature to run around aimlessly checking out bitches. It's written in our genetic code. We can't help it. It will benefit you greatly if you can learn to curb that dog instinct. (Women probably do it, too, but you rarely catch them turning their heads 180 degrees to sniff out some guy's butt walking away down the street.) I know it's hard, but it's for your own good. Try this exercise: When you're out with your wife and Cindy Crawford walks by, do not look away from your wife. Focus. Resisting temptation makes us free.

More to the point: Once you're married, you're not single anymore. This simple sentence has a multitude of ramifications, most significantly that you can't sleep with other women. Bummer. You can't even make out with other women. This is the overriding principle in the vows you freely undertook. You knew about this when you signed up so, when in doubt, refer back to this point. Put a sign on your desk. Keep a card in your wallet. It's a rotten rule, but nobody put a gun to your head, so deal with it, bub.

You will stop "hanging out" like you used to because of the

blessing and the curse of having a wedding ring. Some women are drawn to a wedding ring like moths to a flame. It's not as good as having a cute dog or a whole lot of money when it comes to picking up girls, but it grants you superpowers to talk with women who were previously unapproachable to you. You can talk to these women, you can flirt with them (only if no one—i.e., your wife or any friend of hers—is nearby), but you cannot touch them, especially if they happen to be naked at the time. They know it, and that is why you attract them, you idiot. It is precisely because you don't stand a chance, the ring radiating like neon, that you can drop all the macho pickup posturing and open up and relax. Single women want to get married. Even if you're unavailable you're more accomplished than any Single Guy in the room, simply by being married. That ring is like a diploma in manhood. That's why Vendela is talking to you in the first place.

Some guys get cocky with this newfound superpower and choose to act on it, but it never works out the way they plan. Most of the attraction is the knowledge that for all the flirtatious conversation, the witty banter, you're probably safe. They can drop their guard with your lovable, secure married self. When you show your fangs you're suddenly just like every other guy at the party. Worse, you're a cheating, whoring, lecherous liar. If you think that you could get all these teasing conversations to pay off, think again. Get a divorce and it's gone. Take off the wedding ring and you take off the cape, too. You're unmasked for the mild-mannered chump you are, Clark.

On the other hand, Jim, who is devastatingly handsome and was quite a lady-killer in his day, says the ring seems to have the opposite effect—it's keeping women away in droves. He has never once had a woman say or intimate in any way that she was seeking a meaningless roll in the hay with an unattainable, emotionally involved, married man. His ring might as well be a yellow and black radioactive warning sign, which is its original intent.

It was hard enough when you were single and fidelity was simply a choice you made, not a contract you signed with the devil, with significant penalties for early withdrawal. It doesn't matter how much you love your wife or how hot she is, it couldn't matter less. It's in our nature. Fisher Stevens cheated on Michelle Pfeiffer. Fisher Stevens! You ever get a look at this guy? Michelle Pfeiffer! Questionable judgment call. Hugh Grant ditched Elizabeth Hurley for a blow job from a hooker on Sunset Strip. Elizabeth Hurley! As Jay Leno asked him after the fact, "What were you thinking?"

Marty once said, "Look at any chick, anytime, anywhere in the world, and some guy got tired of fucking her." Yes, you may get tired of banging your wife to the exclusion of anyone and everyone else in the world. But when you realize that if you were to trade her in on a newer model, eventually that deal would start to rust, too. Even trophy wives get old, eventually.

Fidelity is a function of weighing what you stand to lose if you get caught, and how much she will torture you in the process. It's like an AA meeting: one day at a time.

No one new is going to come into your life. Your wife locked the door behind her when she came in. The right thing to do, the noble, virtuous thing, is to fantasize like a lunatic. My friend Danny used to go out to clubs in his work for a record company, and he routinely met attractive young women. He knew at the end of the night he was going to have to stop flirting with these hot little chippies in their hairspray and fuck-me pumps, so he would say good night to the Lolita with this admonition: "I'm going home to my wife now, but I'm going to fuck you tonight."

Most men aren't that lucky. They're not allowed out in clubs where women like this hang out alone at night looking to get you into trouble. They have to make do with fantasies about the girls in the office. In reality, if these guys were single, they probably wouldn't be too interested in dating the girls in the steno pool, wouldn't give them a second thought, but they all get bonus points for not being their wife.

The right thing to do, the good and noble thing, is to masturbate. It's an immutable part of our deal. The divine right of kings. You may make a New Year's resolution every year that this is the year you're going to stop playing with yourself, but get real, man, you need that quality time alone now more than ever. Diddling never had the first thing to do with frequency or availability of sex. It hasn't made you go blind or crazy yet, and it may help keep you sane from here on out. So go ahead and choke that chicken with pride; you might be saving your marriage.

If you think fidelity is a raw deal, remember that she made the same deal. With you. You're the last guy she gets. Look at you, Cary Grant. What a prize you must be to live with. She'll stay with you when you grow more hair in your ears than on your head, when you get fat and funny looking, when you start to fall apart in pieces. What a lucky girl she is.

YOUR IN-LAWS

"A man should never let his wife
visit her mother unattended."
—HONORÉ DE BALZAC

In-laws are another book unto themselves. They, especially mothers-in-law, are the source of more jokes than Polacks. It makes you realize that the reason clichés exist is because they are absolutely, inherently, statistically true. Look these people over carefully. Check their teeth. Kick their tires. Feel the elasticity of their skin. This is the gene pool that made your little wife. Insist on full disclosure of medical and financial records. There is the dowry to consider. All things being equal, an heiress is better than not. (Whatever happened to the dowry? The dowry was the prize package that came with the bride in olden times. Her father said, essentially, if you take my daughter, I'll give you two chickens, a goat, and some linens. That was a damned fine idea if you ask me.)

Spend time with your mother-in-law. Get to know her. Watch her interact with your father-in-law. She will give the lie to every mother-in-law joke you ever heard and never thought was funny. You won't be laughing now, either, Jack. Treat your mother-in-law with all the respect you would show a gorilla in the wild. Remember, she's just like your mother . . . only worse.

Your father-in-law will take some time adjusting to the idea of you. He has seen several contenders come through his front door, all vying for the prize that is his precious daughter. He has seen them come and go. He is hopeful that she has chosen well. He was concerned that she would choose poorly, or not get chosen at all. He wants her off the books, yet he can't help thinking of you as the con man who is raping his little baby girl, his pride and joy, at every opportunity. He shudders to think what the two of you youngsters are doing in private. He will like you better after the ink dries and Daddy's little girl is on your balance sheet, but he will always be watching you like a hawk, waiting for you to fuck up.

Siblings-in-law are basically just more mouths you will have to feed. They're like full-grown children of your own, and they never miss a free meal. Never. Ron liked to joke that he was getting "three for the price of one" when he married the eldest of three sisters. Now he hates to admit that he got "one for the price of three."

Of course, in the exchange of vows, your parents become her in-laws. Pity your unsuspecting wife. There are two possibilities here: Either they love her or they hate her. There is very little gray area with your parents. A typical story is the couple who separated after several years of marriage and the mother-in-law says, "I never liked that man." Revenge, then, comes in the form of getting back together.

One good thing about getting married is that you can now use your wife as a shield to defend against your parents. "Jeez, I'd really love to, Mom, but Karen has something . . ." Make sure you get Karen in on the conspiracy and—like magic!—you're off the hook.

When children enter the picture, your parents become grandparents, and you will wonder why—why, oh why—weren't they more like this when you were growing up.

One other thing you may have to contend with is what to call these people. "Mom and Dad"? "Bob and Sue"? Nothing quite fits. If you're still stuck at "Mr. and Mrs. Jones" after a year, it's a safe bet that things aren't working out the way you'd hoped.

At some point one set of your parents may come to stay with you. This is very bad news indeed. The old expression that "there was never a mother-in-law who remembered that she was once a daughter-in-law" applies here, or they would have had the sense to book a hotel room. You can only be expected to politely survive three days before something gives.

On the other hand you can use this unfortunate occurrence to your advantage and turn the tables on them. Remember when they lorded "My house, my rules" over you? Well—now it's your house and your rules. Insist that they drink milk out of the carton, stay out late, have sex under your roof, smoke dope, and walk around in their underwear scratching themselves.

YOUR FRIENDS

"When a man marries, dies, or turns Hindu,
his best friends hear no more of him."
—PERCY BYSSHE SHELLEY

Once you're married, you may notice that you go out almost exclusively with other couples. Most of your friends are now similarly encoupled. If not, they soon will be. You may begin to look upon your still-single friends as some kind of social pariahs, lessers among equals, and the longer their condition goes unchanged, the more this will become apparent and problematic. They become the "odd man out" or the "fifth wheel." You suddenly want your friends to become half of a couple so that you can still hang out with them. This is the "even number" theory that makes for girl-boy seating at dinner parties.

As a Married Guy, you can now relate to any other married guy anywhere in the world better than the still-single guys who ranked among your best friends not long ago. It's like you graduated from high school, went away to college, and joined an elite fraternity. All the guys in the fraternity went through the same hazing ritual and share some secret knowledge. Meet some stranger on the street and the first thing you ask is, "You married?" "Yup." 'Nuff said. You are brothers for life. You still love your old friends, but they're a little removed from you now, a step behind. They're from the old 'hood, and you've grown out of it. It's almost embarrassing being seen with them. Paraphrasing Prince Charles, singlehood is like a carbuncle on the face of your old friend.

The friends you have at the time you get married are the last friends you will ever make on your own. Henceforth your friends will be married to her friends. He comes with the package that is her. They are "comes withs." Effectively, your wife begins picking out your friends like she picks out your clothes. You basically get what she gives you if your friends don't cut it. It is probably just as well since she's a better judge of character than you, but if you want to keep your old friends, for whatever reason, you better start boxing out like Dennis Rodman.

Your wife, who does not necessarily approve of your miscreant single friends, will take it upon herself to fix them up with some of her chaste and pure girlfriends. She wants them to be as happy as you are. In other words, she wants to put them out of their misery. This fascination begins at the wedding. You hope that your single ushers nail some of her bridesmaids—it makes for an interesting wedding postmortem all around (you get both versions), and there is always the chance that lightning will strike, and you can claim credit for spreading romantic magic like the Ebola virus.

Your friends should be vaguely flattered. The message your wife is sending can be read to mean that "If I was single, and thank God I'm not, I could, in the realm of possibility, consider having that person take me out to dinner, even though he is not, technically, the last man on earth." Another interpretation may well be: "My friend is moving quickly out of her prime childbearing years and, at least, this person looks like a good sperm donor and provider. Better than dying alone, anyway."

You, on the other hand, wouldn't dream of getting into the fix-up game with your friends because, even though you love your friends and want only the best for them, you know them. You know what these lowlifes are capable of—you were one of them not too long ago. If things go badly with the fix-up, at any time, even years later, you will be tarred with the same brush. You might love the guy like a brother, but are you going to stick your dick out on the table for him? Not based on his past behavior. You're asking for trouble.

Then there are your ex-girlfriends. The best thing that could happen would be if they were all suddenly, tragically killed. Since there is little hope of that ever happening and, undoubtedly, an investigation would lead back to you, you will have to walk on eggshells around this most sensitive topic.

If your wife asks a seemingly innocent question about your past life, plead ignorance. Take the Fifth. There are no innocent questions. Don't think just because she expresses an interest in your past that she actually has a healthy normal curiosity. What she has is something more like a vengeful interest in destroying anything from your past that she was not part of. The less said, the better. What do you stand to gain by telling your wife about what some other girl used to do to you? Just leave the names out of it. Say "I'd like it if you'd scratch my back lightly," not "Nancy used to drive me wild when . . ." You see? If you get trapped, you may want to preface every story involving a woman from your past with "A long time ago, in a galaxy far, far away . . ."

Divulge nothing. Remember, for all the millions of questions she will ply you with, trying to trip you up on the stand, there are exactly five answers: Yes, No, I Don't Know, I Don't Recall, and I Don't Understand the Question. You may want to use the familiar form, ending each of the above with "honey," but otherwise these are all the words you need to successfully navigate through a legal deposition or the morass of marriage. It's human nature to want to talk about it, but human nature only gets humans into trouble, so shut your yap and you'll live to be a happy, funny-smelling old man.

You may want to make a horse's head of all your exes and just turn the whole lot of them into one huge nameless, faceless compilation. In the misguided pursuit of something like honesty and openness, you will have to cough up at least one name. It's like ratting out your accomplice in a plea bargain arrangement to lesser charges.

For the record, nobody ever did anything as well as your wife. Nobody else even medaled in any event of remotest importance. The first runner-up finished something like fifth. It will bode well if none of these also-rans gets invited to the wedding. (You don't want any of the guys she did unspeakable things with there either, smirking behind your back like they know something you don't. Bastards! At least you have the last laugh, for now.)

Men and women should be advised that their history begins the moment they meet, unless they choose otherwise. Honesty is a policy but, as old Nietzsche says: "One should never know too precisely whom one has married." If you have already given up the game . . . all that is water under the bridge. Ancient history. A formative experience. The people involved are like fossils from some distant, unrecognizable past. Her ex-boyfriends did almost everything with her that you did with your ex-girlfriends. Somewhere there is at least one guy you owe a grudging thank-you to. You know that somehow she got to be good in bed, but you don't want to know how. Don't ask, don't tell.

Some of your friends may be a divisive force in the marriage. These are the guys your wife disapproves of and/or vice versa. They're your friends, she's your wife; they didn't marry her, you did. You don't have to choose, but you don't have to put gasoline and a match together either. You'll have one or more "Guy" friends who you begin to see more or less strictly on a *mano a mano* basis, never the twain shall meet. This is what the Preamble to the Constitution calls "insuring domestic tranquillity."

You will roll your eyes at your friends when they tell you some shit about their wives. Like you don't know all about it, Jack. There is only one wife. You'll be tempted to get into a game of one-upmanship. Under no circumstance should you be subjected to more than five minutes of some other guy's wife's bullshit. You already bought your own cow.

CIGARS

"A husband is a man who has made one mistake
but keeps learning from it all his life."

When a woman wants to get married, there are a lot of things that she is willing to tolerate and accept. She will not be so tolerant or accepting of these same things after she has bagged her quarry. A cigar is not always a cigar, for example. You used to smoke them and she used to put up with them when you were single. It was one of your faults she learned to love or at least accept. She thought cigars were cute. Once you're married, all that is over.

Henceforth, you will be smoking almost exclusively outdoors. You may find yourself being scrubbed down until all traces of the offending odor are removed, and forced to submit to an inspection before being permitted back into your own bed. You'll wind up walking the dog in order to smoke a cigar, like all the other married guys in your neighborhood. That's what they're doing. They're not taking the dog out per se, they're escaping from their better halves so they can enjoy a decent smoke. Killing two birds with one stone. The dog is a prop, something to do as long as you're up, someone to talk to as long as you're out. Married Guys nod to each other in silent recognition when they're out smoking, like Shriners at a party. It is a fraternity of not exactly henpecked men, but resigned men, men who face reality daily, men who go to war every morning. They would all rather be inside, in their dens, their caves, with all their familiar things around them, manning the remote control with a big glass ashtray and a snifter of brandy to keep them company but, as they say in baseball, a walk is as good as a hit.

My man Kramer has been put into the following box by his wife: If you smoke a cigar, I won't have sex with you tonight; if you don't, I will. (By which she means "I might.") It's that simple. You choose. Mind you, I like cigars, a lot, but I love sex. As a Single Guy that's not even a decision. Suck on a burning, stinking weed stick or suck on a live nude girl. Single Guy will take the live nude girl every time. But old married Kramer, who, admittedly, likes cigars much more than I, splits his week down the middle. A couple of *robustos,* a couple of romps with the old lady. No one is exactly happy, but they're not especially unhappy about the compromise. If he smokes, they're both off the hook.

Going to a cigar bar has some of the same satisfaction of cheating on your wife. It's like a trip to a whorehouse. Men discreetly puffing on illegal Cubans and sipping on brown liquids, speaking in hushed tones, eyes down, trying to maintain their anonymity in the dark as they perpetrate a victimless crime. There is honor among thieves in this place.

Smoking in public now requires protective cover. If a bunch of the boys settle into an after-dinner smoker, at least you have safety in numbers and peer pressure as an alibi. "I had to smoke, honey. I couldn't tell them 'my wife won't let me.'" Cigars are practically the last bastion of maleness left, and women are starting to move in on that action, too. This is progress?

RELAXING

"Marriage is a feminist plot
to add to a man's responsibilities
and subtract from his rights."

For a small piece of paper, it carries a lot of weight. Forget about money or fidelity and all that other shit. A wedding license can do some serious shit to your head. My man Otis says that the first thing that happens is your ability to relax disappears. You are never going to be alone again, which almost sounds like it was part of the original equation you accounted for when you agreed to be together forever, but there is no clear way to describe the real consequences of such a decision. Said differently, she will never leave you alone again.

After a sixteen-hour day at the office or breaking rocks in the quarry, slaying corporate dragons or whatever it is you do, there is only the remotest possibility that you are going to come home, drop your shit on the couch, and unwind in the peace and tranquillity of bachelor solitude. You'll want to settle into some Al Bundy quality time with ESPN and a cold beer, but you are going to have to be nurturing and caring and sharing about the day you are trying so hard to forget. Her good intentions will be your undoing, and there's nothing you can do about it because most women don't understand a man's need to be alone. Not privacy, per se, she wants as much privacy as you do, but the primal urge just to be left the fuck alone to scratch your ass and watch the goddamn game. Try to make her see the logic in this sentence: "I worship the ground you walk on. Now go away." Carl Reiner told me that the beauty of marriage is "You can eat an egg salad sandwich with your wife. Single guys should never eat egg salad."

Otis says you have to get your wife into your sports-viewing regimen as soon as possible. It is incumbent upon you to teach her the hit-and-run, the give-and-go, the two-minute drill. Some chicks already come fully loaded from the factory with the knowledge, they like sports and require little or no reconditioning. They had a brother or a father (or some guy you don't even want to know about) who exposed them to the epic struggles played out on grassy fields and wooden courts. Maybe she was a cheerleader. (In which case she might still have her letterman sweater and pleated skirt. Ask her.)

Sally Jenkins, in her very funny book *Men Will Be Boys,* claims that "Modern Woman Is a Creature of Enormous Complexity," and is capable of understanding and enjoying sports. "The conclusion here is obvious: Women are pigs too! But we are female pigs." This is a good woman.

Conversely, in her not very funny at all book *How to Talk to Your Husband—How to Talk to Your Wife,* Patti McDermott, M.F.C.C., has a chapter titled "In My Book Watching a Football Game Together Doesn't Qualify as Intimacy." (First of all, what the fuck is "M.F.C.C." all about, does anybody know?) Although she acknowledges that men don't like to talk about things, she wants to talk about everything. More important, she knows nothing about football. Or men. Watching a football game together is like letting her into your secret world, a world of nonverbal communication, a world of unspoken intimacy.

You may have to reciprocate by showing appreciation for women's sports—gymnastics, ice skating, ballet, shit like that. Fortunately, they only show up at the Olympics, every four years or so, and you don't have to put up with too much of it. Also fortunately, these little girls all wear leotards and micro miniskirts when they shake their moneymakers. It's better than soft-core porn on cable and you seem like such a sensitive person for watching. Pretend not to notice, you randy old man.

If you don't want to talk about something, she will think you're locking her out of your life. The worse it is, the more she wants to know about it. If you talk about it, you can't relax. If she wants to talk to you about her day and you don't, you're really fucked, because you're actually going to have to listen and pay attention to her. You're required to do more than nod appropriately. You must ask questions, empathize, emote. If you don't want to listen to what you loosely call "her bullshit" and actually have the misplaced chutzpah to say so, there is going to be blood on the walls. Sometimes "yes dear" just won't cut it. Damned if you do, fucked if you don't; you're not relaxing either way.

Some guys become workaholics as a means of relaxing. They get some computer games loaded into the office mainframe, bring in a Watchman, keep a bottle in the bottom desk drawer—it's the next best thing to being home alone. If you have kids, the relative chaos of the office will seem like a church service or a holiday in Hawaii by comparison.

Men and women account for time differently. Harlan would spend the whole day Sunday with Suzie, doing couple stuff together—brunch, shopping, taking in a chick flick. When they got home he'd flip on the late game on TBS and she'd flip out: "We never spend any time together!"

You must establish hobbies early in the going, or you'll never get to enjoy them. As it stands, you may have to fight for this piece of turf. If you didn't have a regular softball game when you met your wife, you're not going to get one now without a discussion.

If you're not a duffer yet, you should seriously consider golf, as it is something you can do with other guys who are basically killing a few hours away from the little missus, commiserating with each other by drinking beer in the open air. There is no exercise involved. It is the most frustrating game ever conceived but it will still seem like the warden has granted you parole. Golf is group therapy for men.

Do not get your wife into golf. If this can't be avoided, never, ever play with her. You should not feel that going golfing with your wife will allow you to share more. It will only allow you to fight more. You'll want to instruct her on her follow-through; it's in your nature, even if you've never broken 100. She'll want to drive a sand wedge up your nose. If you give her a good-natured hard time about three-putting the 14th hole, she will make you pay for it later. Seriously, why can't a woman be more like a man?

I love guys who are in training for the triathlon. They've got to really hate their home life to put themselves through this torture. The triathlon is to be considered only after all other resources have been exhausted.

If you travel in business you get some time alone and then guess what happens? You miss your wife. You can't wait to get home and start the cycle over again. You can't win for losing. That is the marriage story in a nutshell.

Be judicious in your reliance on hobbies. Ralph Kramden pushed Alice too far and had to take her and Trixie bowling with Norton. He might as well have worn a dress out to the lanes.

AROUND
THE HOUSE

"Of course it is quite possible to marry for love, but I suspect that a good many bachelors marry so that they may not have to bother about the washing anymore. That, anyhow, will be one of the reasons with me. 'I offer you,' I shall say, 'my hand and heart— and the washing.'"

—A. A. MILNE

Harvey is a sixty-ish man, wise from decades of marriage. He watched in disbelief as his aspiring son-in-law tried to help clear the plates early in his relationship with his daughter. The young man, in his eager effort to make a good impression by showing his participation, broke a plate in the kitchen, sending food flying everywhere. Then he made a weak attempt to help clean up while his mother-in-law started screaming something in Spanish to the phalanx of housekeepers. When the poor lad returned to the dining room Harvey told him the following: "Why even try?"

There are some men who are genuinely good at household stuff, but for the most part we're hopelessly inexperienced and otherwise helpless. They, on the other hand, have been playing "house" behind our backs for years and should be more than able to carry on without our help. Nevertheless, despite the enormous discrepancy between our relative abilities in this field of endeavor, your wife will expect you to pull your own weight around the house. Rob Becker answers this for all men, and for all time: "Yeah? Go program the VCR."

I can cook, for example, but I can't do laundry. Here's how you get out of it: As we discussed in the chapter titled "Compatibility" you have a responsibility to let your wife know, early in the relationship, that laundry is a personality deficiency. You have no aptitude for it whatsoever. She, a woman, being a suspicious person by nature, will think you're trying to shirk your husbandly duties. Let her think whatever she wants, you can prove it. Do everything (whites, colors, brights, darks) on hot and hard (press the button that says "frappe"), then toss the whole mess in the turbo dryer at the highest setting for at least one hour. By the time it's done you will have shrunk, bled, or otherwise destroyed a lot of it. How hard can it be to fuck up the laundry? She will carry on for a while, call you an idiot, maybe even try to teach you how to do it right. Murder a couple more of her silk things, replace anything you ruined, and you're off the hook for the rest of your life. Burt Reynolds says, "Marriage is about the most expensive way for the average man to get laundry done."

I also can't make a bed by myself. I kind of like doing it with a woman, the morning after, if you will. I like it better when a woman does it for me. A woman I'm paying to do it for me. A woman whose first language is not necessarily English. A maid is the best investment you will ever make. She is a genius when it comes to cleaning. It may technically be "unskilled" labor, but you couldn't do it, college boy. She knows the difference between all those cleaning products at the supermarket that all look alike to you. No matter how poor you are, you can always afford to hire some Third World woman to clean up your mess.

My father is a brilliant man. He attended Yale, became a leader in his field of business, but his most lasting achievement was inventing the "Guy." Pop knows his personal shortcomings, and one of them is his complete, utter inability to do anything around the house. He's a train wreck. There is nothing he can do without breaking something in the process. He understands this and has dealt with it, and we can all learn from his experience. He has a "Guy" who does everything. My dad doesn't screw in a light bulb without a Guy. He loves to boast about what a great Guy he's got, that he's got the best Guy in every field of endeavor. You can't even get an appointment with his Guy without a personal recommendation, but he's willing to share his encyclopedic knowledge of Guys with his friends. When in doubt, call the Guy.

Why even try?

THINGS THAT YOU
USED TO DO

"A woman worries about her future
until she gets a husband,
while a man never worries about the future
until he gets a wife."

—ANON.

As Single Guy, your plans were about as fixed as the wind. You did what you wanted. Now you have to check with your wife if you want to do something that might be fun and simultaneously not involve her. Simply put, you have been stripped of your manhood. As we shall see in future chapters, you basically married your mother. Your ability to "get up and go" just got up and went. You find that you increasingly say "I have to" instead of "I want to." Being responsible is a drag. Being irresponsible is fun. Was fun. Responsibility makes us free. Great.

This is not to say that you have lost your taste for doing fun things, but you can't do them spontaneously anymore. There are no more last-minute tickets to Laker games. You won't be ready for them if they become available. Mickey said, "I'm as spontaneous as I ever was, I just need more advance notice nowadays." Spontaneity is the thing that defined your bachelorhood—the complete ability to ditch everything for something more fabulous that came along without warning. After all, spontaneity has its place and time, too.

You may notice that nightclubs and discos have become places that you don't go to anymore because they are crowded, loud, dark, and smoky. Those are precisely the reasons you used to like clubs, but now these places just make your clothes smell bad and give you a headache, like rock music does. (And it is increasingly apparent that your musical tastes are gradually lining up in the camp of "Songs I Can Understand the Words To.")

You won't want to stay out too late, drinking and smoking too much or taking drugs, because there is no prize in the box of Cracker Jacks for you to find at the end of the night. The reason you drank too much and did all that other regrettable stuff was mostly so you could meet women who, on a good night, might let you get some. Without them, you would have gone to med school and made something of yourself but, after all those hours spent on barstools chatting up the bimbo nation, at least now you know the difference between single malt and blended scotch whiskey.

You no longer have the need to impress your wife with your savoir faire. The simple fact that you're married now will lead inexorably to a simultaneous diminution in your appetite for nightlife. This phenomenon may be explained by some kind of Jungian "synchronicity," but probably not. Unless you and your ball and chain are chronic booze hounds, you probably don't want to see your Golden Years spent together on barstools. Do you know the Louis Jourdan song "What's the Use of Getting Sober (When You're Gonna Get Drunk Again)"? Now you might as well ask yourself the opposite question: "What's the use of getting drunk?"

Your clubbing days are going into the closet with your bell-bottoms. First you fall behind the curve, then out with the in crowd, then off the bus altogether. By the time you get to a hot new place you've heard about, the beautiful people will have moved on and you'll wonder what all the hubbub was about in the first place. There are no more late shows in your immediate future. You'll start leaving ballgames in the seventh inning.

My friend Sardo once told me the sweetest, saddest, most sexist thing in the world. We were at a party with some models, splashing around in a Jacuzzi. He left early to go back to his room where his wife and angelic sleeping kid awaited him. The next day he said that being married means that you know where you're going to end up at the end of the night. There's no point to hanging out at the bar or the party waiting to see what happens next. The third act is already written on every night out. It's like watching the Harlem Globetrotters play—but suddenly realizing you're the Washington Generals. So, the Sardo Principle goes, if you're not going to get anywhere with your act, why bother dusting it off to impress somebody you ultimately don't care about. This was sweet because he loved his wife and was happy to be going back to her at the end of any given evening; sad because he was losing his soul in the process of loving his wife; and sexist because his reasoning says that if you can't sleep with a woman, why bother talking to her?

If you go out with some of your Single Guy friends you can actually serve a useful function: You can fetch. As Married Man, you are beaver bait. You open them with your disarming Married Man rap, take them out of their game, then hand them over to the relief pitcher to close the deal. You do this because (a) you want to help your friends with acts of selfless generosity, (b) you want to keep your chops sharp, keep in practice just to make sure you still got it, and (c) because you've made your friend swear to tell you everything that happens. Every nasty little detail, every position, etc. You want to have an e-mail that says "Smell my finger."

FOREVERNESS

"I couldn't see the point of tying myself down
to a middle aged woman with four children,
even though the woman was my wife
and the children were my own."
—JOSEPH HELLER

hink about all the best friends you've had in your life. Think about all the stuff you've had in your life. What's the oldest thing you own? Your longest-standing commitment? A thirty-year mortgage is like buying a season subscription to the opera compared to getting married. Everything else you buy has an expiration date on it, but your marriage is the only thing you have that is set to expire when one of you does.

My man Wex says that this sense of time is the biggest thing. Most men tend to first look at the concept of permanence in marriage as having to do with one thing: their dick. There is not a married man alive who has not said "This is the last woman I'm ever going to sleep with," or words to that effect. That turns out to be the least of it. The vast expanse of time between now and The End is much bigger than your dick. Single guys don't buy green bananas, they don't like to make dates more than ten days away, and they almost can't see beyond the next fiscal quarter. Married guys think of short-term planning as having to do with the next decade, they buy wine futures. Their idea of long-term planning is insurance policies, side-by-side burial plots, the Twelfth of Never. You aren't in a hurry anymore. You're living your future. It ain't gonna get that much different.

George Bernard Shaw said, "Marriage is popular because it combines the maximum of temptation with the maximum of opportunity." If you want to cheat on your wife, there's no hurry. She ain't going anywhere. There's always another day to stab Caesar. She'll still be around, waiting for you to cheat on her next year.

She is always there. For better and for worse. It's enough to make you cry. There is virtually no getting rid of her. This will undoubtedly come as comfort to you during the better and worse times, but there will be moments, lots and lots of them, during the in-between times that she's going to drive you nuts. Ball and chain is right, my friend. You might as well staple yourselves together. You're going to want to be alone so badly you'll do what all married men have done before you throughout time: hide in the bathroom. You'll find more stuff that you can do in an eighteen-square-foot room than you previously thought possible. The Nintendo Game Boy was invented by a man who wanted to be alone. So were crossword puzzles. And magazines. My father has cable TV and a Discman in his bathroom. He has spent four hours a day in there for the past twenty years. It's his personal bunker. This is what we have to look forward to.

THE DEAL

"If women didn't exist, all the money in the world
would have no meaning."
—ARISTOTLE ONASSIS

An ex-girlfriend of mine was friendly with the first Mrs. Steven Spielberg. She told me that for Christmas one year, Steven gave Amy Irving carte blanche at a very expensive boutique in Los Angeles called Maxfield Blue. One night at dinner I related this to my father and an old friend of his, both of whom are rich and successful. I finished explaining that Amy could get whatever she wanted, as much as she wanted, whenever she wanted, and waited for their shocked response. They considered each other for a moment and then turned to face me. "Yeah. So?" I tried again to explain that this was unlimited access to the most expensive store in town, but they were still unimpressed. I was confused. I was waiting for the other shoe to fall, so I said, "All right. I'll bite. What's the deal?"

My father, all full of wisdom, then explained everything in three words. Here they are: "That's the deal."

Steven didn't give Amy anything.

Now do you get it?

A fool and his money are soon married. Danny Thomas said: "Anyone who thinks marriage is a 50/50 proposition doesn't understand anything about women, or fractions." Your wife of five minutes now technically owns you. She is worth half the value of the partnership, and she's got the pussy, so there you have it. She owns 51 percent of you. She owns 51 percent of anything you ever order in a restaurant. Some call this pussy-whipped. Others call this a merger, a friendly takeover. You will be the CFO to her CEO in the newly formed company, but make no mistake: She's the new boss. In this regard, marriage is like any other job: It helps if you like your boss.

You may occasionally find it necessary to initiate a temporary spending freeze at home. This will take place immediately, you tell the company in a sternly worded interoffice memo. You're cutting back on wasteful practices, and henceforth will be checking expense reports with a fine-tooth comb. Until she says different. What are you going to do? Fire her? She is your boss, man. Besides which, she needed those shoes. You didn't specify that the draconian cutbacks you outlined in your sternly worded memo (a) applied to her or (b) included necessities, besides, (c) she didn't read your sternly worded memo until it was too late to return the pumps and (d) they were on sale. (Luckily for you, your wife has never seen a pair of shoes that wasn't on sale.)

For men, shopping is a one-dimensional exercise. Go to store. Buy thing. Go home. We are soldiers on a very specific mission. We want to accomplish our goal and return to base as quickly as possible, put the experience behind us so we can get on with the more important matters that fall to us men. Women, if you don't know this yet, are like butterflies, floating from store to store on a lifelong shopping spree. Social anthropologists credit this to their historical role as "gatherers." Occasionally they go in search of one item, but they never come back with just one. The more they acquire throughout their lifetime, the more they just kind of float in the ether of retail. They stop to admire little things in the window wherever they go. They stop to say "gorgeous" about things that are very similar to things they already own. Shopping is an end in itself. We believe that my mother could find shopping opportunities in the Gobi desert. She possesses a bottomless will when it comes to buying things. She gets stronger as the day goes on. She couldn't tell you who played in the last World Series, but she knows how late Saks stays open. It's amazing.

Your wife will give you things you already have. One example of this is if you are the only breadwinner in the household (and this is not to denigrate the importance of housework and child rearing. My mother hastens to point out that there is value in these things, too), she will go out, spend your money to buy you a present, and expect you to thank her for it. If she already asked you what you wanted for a present, the only difference between buying it yourself and receiving it as a gift is the wrapping paper. You're thanking her for saving you a trip to the store.

As soon as you have children you are on the hook forever. For ever. They enter the world with a cry that costs you around five thousand dollars. Every time they cry for the next twenty or thirty years it will cost you a grand or two. Even if you save a small fortune by sending the kid to public school, you still have food and clothing, toys and books, allowance, doctors, endless lessons, sports gear, their friends' birthday presents, camp, a car, insurance, and on and on and on, ad infinitum.

Conservatively, a child costs one million dollars through college. You have no say in this matter whatsoever. You work for them from the moment of their conception until the moment of your demise. Parenthood is a lot easier to get into than out of. You can't choose not to send Junior to the orthodontist for braces or your kid will look like Howdy Doody and people will point at you in shame when you pass in the street.

There is no adjustment for inflation, and all of it, every single piece of crap you buy for twenty years or more, is completely and utterly disposable. They want things they don't even want, and you, you big dummy, get these things for them. For some reason you trust their judgment on this stuff that they are pointing at and screaming about, knowing that these people would eat candy for every meal if they could. Gallagher says the reason God made kids cute is so you don't kill 'em. At their college graduation, you will have nothing to show for your bottomless investment in planned obsolescence. Thank God income rises to meet expenses.

STUFF

"By all means marry. If you get a good wife
you will become happy; and if you get a bad one
you will become a philosopher."

—SOCRATES

You're going to be separated from some of your stuff. Keeping in mind that it's only 49 percent yours now, or, said differently, only 49 percent of it is yours now. Someday, perhaps inevitably, she's going to throw out your favorite pair of beat-up old sneakers or your stereo boxes or something, probably to make room for more of her stuff. She might not consult you on these minor household matters, either. One day you'll look for some stuff you actually need and it will be gone and that will be that.

The redecoration of your life begins even before the wedding. Think about Bruno Kirby's wagon wheel table in *When Harry Met Sally* . . . Out. Anything even remotely associated with another woman from your past life: out.

Any remnant of your bachelor past will slowly be exorcised from your life together like some Orwellian Bekins, until your glory days are but a dim memory, like a movie you saw once, a long time ago. Get a safe-deposit box or one day you'll find yourself in a padded cell, trying to remember that halcyon time, because you have no artifacts left in your possession to prove who you used to be. My friend Steve's wife, Pam, put an ad in the local weekly paper and sold his black leather sofa to some guy on the terms that he had to cart it away by five o'clock (i.e., before Steve came home and kiboshed the deal). Anything that is black and leather is going to be "disappeared," like a political dissident in Chile.

You can never discuss any of this with your wife, or she won't be your wife for long. It has long been understood that she doesn't understand your stuff. Lucy threw out Ricky's favorite shirt and the same scene has been repeating itself in every family home across the nation ever since. It is a historical fact. A rite of passage.

Referring back to the "man evolved from dogs" theory, you must mark your territory like a dog. Eventually you'll establish a bunker mentality, like my father. His room ("my quarters") is guarded by barbed wire and attack dogs. It's the biggest mess of junk you ever saw in your life. There is nothing especially valuable or important in there, but it's his and he's not going to throw any of it away without a fight. He has to move something out of the way so that one person can sit down, but it keeps people (i.e., the riffraff) out, and he likes it that way. The rest of the house is spotless, but his room is off limits to my mother and the invading hordes of well-intentioned cleaning people. Most young married couples don't have the luxury of a bunker, so sleep with one eye open. Beware, brother, beware.

If you hadn't gotten married, you'd have a BMW motorcycle, a bitchin' stereo, and lots of other cool stuff. You'd have everything you ever wanted, but you don't need any of that shit now, something your wife will remind you from time to time. Don Rickles came back from a European vacation with his wife, Barbara, convinced that every shopkeeper from Paris to Moscow thought his name was "You-don't-need-that-Don."

SEX

"Marriage is the price men pay for sex.
Sex is the price women pay for marriage."

—ANON.

By the time you are in a position to get engaged or married, chances are you will have had most of the best sex you'll ever have in your life. Especially with that woman. You may scale those heights again, but the theory of diminishing sexual returns states it will not be with the same regularity of past endeavors. There is also the chance that you didn't marry your all-time sexual all-star, in which case it's possible that you really did reach your sexual peak at eighteen. Savor those times. Commit them to memory. Your married sex life is like the sequel to a cool picture, or a remake. It's still pretty cool, but not as good as the original. Not a goddamn thing you can do about it except cheat on your wife—but that's cheating.

My sister says that if you put a penny in a jar every time you make love with your future wife before you get married, and take a penny out of the jar every time you make love to her after you get married, you'll never go broke. A lot of love is wasted before marriage that could be put to good use afterward.

Every guy I know says, "No way, man. Not me. We love sex. We do it all the time. That shit's never going to change, not with us." Posturing aside, the guy is always wrong. First of all, the hunt is over.

You've already bagged your quarry, now you gotta deal with it. Nobody is out to prove their sexual virtuosity. You've been with this woman for a while by now, and trying to recapture that first date/falling in love magic just keeps getting further away. You love her more than ever, but there's nothing even remotely immoral about it now, so why get all worked up?

Being married is like having a lifetime subscription to *Playboy*—except that you get the same centerfold every month, and pretty soon she's not twenty-two anymore. By the time your subscription runs out, she looks like the horny grandmother in the *Playboy* cartoons, with her tits halfway down to her hips like two socks full of nickels. By then, you'll want to have sex exclusively with anyone else but her. Here's a great one-liner from Rodney Dangerfield: "Last time I made love to my wife nothing was happening so I said to her, 'What's the matter? You can't think of anybody either?' "

The joke is ultimately on your randy single friends, who are the hares. They may be in and out of hot relationships, hitting the long ball on a one-night stand or a romantic weekend, but they will hit cold streaks. Everything will come crashing down, a miracle of bad timing, all at once, and then they've got nothing but the comfort of self-love. A season-long slump. You, on the other hand, you lucky married dog, are like the tortoise. You're not swinging for the fences anymore, slugger. Consistency is your hallmark. Slow and steady wins the race.

Frequency aside, the sheer firepower of the sex itself is going to gradually cool. There is no urgency to turn in an all-star performance. She'll be back tomorrow for a rematch. You're less likely to do it in exotic places; hell, even the other furniture in your house is going to look exotic two months after you were feeding each other cake. It's natural. Your taste for hot sex is going to eventually go the way of your head-first slide into second—you still know how, but it just gets harder to get down and do it as you get older. You know the story going in. You've seen the other team. You know her moves. There are no big surprises out there. Now it comes down to the execution of your game plan.

You may come to think that any other sex that anybody else is having anywhere else has got to be more interesting than whatever you're doing. You'll beg your single friends for tales of derring-do at the end of the weekend—or beg them to stop once they get started. (Incidentally, you won't ask your married friends for—nor will they volunteer—any information about their love lives. It would not be that different from yours anyway.) Part of this is just the "other man's grass" principle at work, but it happens to be true. The other man's grass is sometimes always greener.

A woman's "Wifely Duties" have become increasingly subject to interpretation. In the good old days you took what you wanted. Now that's called rape or spousal abuse or some other shit. Now if the Mrs. turns to you in your moment of need and desire and says "you got it last week," you ain't getting any. You're simultaneously screwed and not getting screwed.

"Honey?"

"No." End of story. No blow job. No nothin'. Use your dick, go to jail.

You will someday find yourself in the surreal position of calling your wife, the woman with whom you share a bed every night, to make a date to have sex. After a week of "I was here, she was there, we were tired," it may be the only way to get together. Nothing wrong with that either. Two people getting together is a good thing. Dates are a good thing. They give you the momentary impression that you're still working for it.

Most of the poor fellows I spoke with said their sex life was not bad. Mike said that you simply settle into a routine—once a week, once a month, whatever. It's understood. Tim Allen says: "The good thing is that reduced frequency just sort of creeps up on you, and stays with you, like midriff bulge." You have the power to control the frequency with something called "romance." Check it out.

Sex is part of the job of married life. Much as you don't like to think of it in this light, sex is work. Do your job, man. If your sex life ain't happening to your satisfaction, you only have to look in the mirror to find the problem. She's open to suggestion. At least she used to be. Eat her on the dining room table with a little Cool Whip. Light candles. Take a bath together. Be the fucking Man. Tear her bodice off. Give her a massage. These broads like romance, all that flowers and lovey-dovey shit. Give and ye shall receive. Give the people what they want. Do your job or you'll be out of a job when she calls in a specialist to do it for you.

BLOW JOBS

"If you ladies knew what we were really thinking you'd never stop slapping us."
—RICHARD JENI

There is no mystery about what happens to blow jobs. They dwindle and eventually go away. This is part of the cost of acquisition that all women voluntarily subject themselves to, then all but abandon once their objective has been attained. You knew this was too good to last.

If a woman should doubt that the above is true, that blow jobs decrease in frequency over time the longer you're married, tell her this: Prove it.

Blow jobs are the doggie biscuits of your married life. Just as you will likely never get her flowers for "no reason," so it goes with blow jobs. You will get them for being a good dog/husband. Not to be too crass, but buying her gifts will get you one. Molly McGee says that "If a man buys a woman a present for no reason, there's usually a good reason," and this is as good a reason as any. Good dog. Make-up flowers might get you one. Your birthday, yes; hers, no. Wedding anniversary is a coin toss. You should stress the point that Christmas is the spirit of giving, and receiving.

It's also understood that you only get so many blow jobs per year. Imagine yourself in a giant game of Monopoly. Blow jobs are like Get Out of Jail Free cards, yours to use at any time, but judiciously. Asking for head is like calling an audible at the line of scrimmage, at your discretion, meant to confound the prevent defense.

Nothing's free, though. Believe it. There's the joke about the little girl who says "Mommy, last night I came into your room and Daddy was putting his pee-pee in you. What were you doing?"

"We were making babies, honey."

"But then Daddy put his pee-pee in your mouth, what were you doing?"

"Mommy was making jewelry, dear." Quid pro quo.

Sexual researchers at Masters and Johnson are looking into the correlation between giving and receiving head. Assuming that you want to continue to receive blow jobs for the rest of your life (as did your father before you, though this is too scary a thought for this book), it stands to reason you should be ready and willing to give head for the rest of your life. This is a fine and noble thought. It is a romantic and loving thought. Now. When you and your wife are reasonably young and good looking and physically fit. Now go outside and look at some old ladies, women in their fifties, sixties, seventies, eighties. Pick a few of them. Now imagine that your wife is going to look more or less like these people. Now imagine going down on them. (Of course, you have to imagine that you are their age, too.) Can't do it, can you, tough guy? Now you know what happens to blow jobs and why you don't see a lot of love scenes in movies with old actors.

On the other hand, your interest in the very same blow job is going to dwindle until it eventually may go away along with her desire to provide same. My friend Marcus used to love it when his wife would proffer a little oral foreplay when he wasn't expecting it—maybe when he was watching TV or sleeping, or whatever. Now he finds himself looking down at his well-meaning spouse, saying, "What are you doing? You're getting it all wet!"

"A soiled baby with a neglected nose
cannot be conscientiously regarded
as a thing of beauty."

—MARK TWAIN

Getting a woman pregnant is the easiest thing in the world. You don't have to pass a test. Hell, you don't even have to take a test. You don't have to have any special skills, as if achieving an orgasm was a talent. Not achieving an orgasm is a talent. "Motility" only rhymes with "ability." Some people can do it despite taking FDA-approved countermeasures. Almost everybody likes the process. However, after spending your entire single life seeking sexual fulfillment without accidentally inseminating your partner, now the exact opposite set of rules is in effect: You want to knock up the old lady. When you throw out the birth control, you've turned the corner from recreational sex to procreational sex.

When are you ready to have children? A lot of men are reluctant to become fathers because they aren't through being children. Some people pick a date to begin to conceive a child. They put it on their list of things to do. Somewhere between picking up the dry cleaning and calling the plumber is a Post-it note to fertilize your wife's egg. At this point sex is reduced to an errand whose goal is nothing less than the continuation of the human species.

When you're single, you think that people who are "trying" to conceive children really have it good. No. Wrong. Now the snooze alarm on her biological clock is broken. You're just a cheap sex toy for your woman's pleasure and you serve a single purpose—you are a sperm donor. That's all you're good for. An erection in Italian shoes. Don't waste your energy helping with the dishes, Johnny Appleseed, Madame requires the pleasure of your company in the boudoir, pronto! "I dunno," said Stewart, who was "trying." "When she says hump, I hump."

Who says romance is dead?

Did you ever take a good look at these people? Do they look especially happy because they're having sex on a more regular basis than at any time since they first met? Do they seem to be enjoying themselves? Do they look like they're having fun? No, no, and no. They look tired and irritable. They're cranky and sore. They have taken all the fun out of the process, turning the one sacredly fun thing in the world into work. It's like working a second job. My friend Jake's grandfather-in-law called him up and in a very businesslike fashion said, "Son, if you can't get her pregnant, I'm gonna get someone in there who *can* do the job."

There is nothing sexier than a woman with a thermometer stuck in her pussy, trying to determine the optimal moment for you to fertilize her egg. Schwing! (Not!) It's a thankless task, this insemination business, and, though you hate to admit it, if you didn't really have to be there at the conception, you might just pass. Phone it in.

Some guys, when they hear that you're "trying," will jump to the conclusion that your "boys can't swim." (For the record: My boys can peel the paint off wood.) This shit never happens to those poor, uneducated, undernourished, high-cholesterol, Third World huddled masses types. And what if it's true? Is it a comment on you or your manliness?

If at first you don't succeed, try, try again.

Q: What's the difference between a pregnant woman and a terrorist?

A: You can negotiate with a terrorist.

When you finally do get the good news that the experiment was a success and you are now collectively pregnant, you will greet it like you just split the atom or won Olympic gold. It happens a hundred million times every year, and yet somehow every couple treats it like they performed a miracle or a David Copperfield magic trick.

When you are going to have a baby, your wife is said to be "expecting." You, on the other hand, are simply "waiting." She is "in the family way," while you are merely *in* the way. After you plant the seed you have nothing to do. Becoming a father is basically a show-up job for you, a clock-killer. Maybe you'll drive the car to the hospital, whereupon you might participate in the birth as a spectator. Face it, you're a bystander in the whole project. You're just window dressing at doctor's appointments, but your name is dirt if you don't show up. You're essentially a walker. It has come to this.

You will suddenly become aware of all the little children in the world, and how they no longer seem like messy, doughy little noise makers. Mommies and Daddies pushing their rug rats around in strollers through crowded restaurants are blessed, not burdened, as you would have believed when you were a callous Single Guy, or even a Barren Man, when you wanted the monsters to go play elsewhere. Anywhere. Outside, in traffic, whatever.

Sex during pregnancy is going to be the final frontier for many of you, the true test of your manhood. Over steaks and scotch one night, a friend named Harlan got into an extended discourse on sex during pregnancy with some of the boys, all single, and we couldn't handle it. You could show this gang a snuff film and we would be okay, but this subject matter was way too creepy for us. We just didn't want to hear it. Since almost nobody in their right mind would actually, knowingly, pick up a pregnant woman to have sex with, even if she was available and/or willing, and/or Demi Moore, this is a bridge you're going to have to jump off when you get to it. Your wife may be radiant and glowing and all that crap, but she's mostly going to be fat, sick, moody, and even more demanding than usual—and there's not a goddamn thing you can do about it. After a while she's going to care a lot less about shaving her legs and her everything else she shaved that you never wanted to know about, except that it has always been shaved and soft and lovely for your personal pleasure. By the seventh month she's going to throw out the book on personal grooming. If you see an eight-month-pregnant woman in a bikini, it's a sight you won't easily forget.

And then in a private moment, a friend named Lucas said that he loved having sex with his pregnant wife. He's the kind of guy who likes to tinker with things and find out how they work, so the changing geometry of entry positions was something amusing to him. But the thing he liked best was that his wife was "like a ripe fruit"—wet and juicy. And there is the unexpected bonus that her breast size will increase arithmetically with everything else.

Another friend said, "She finally got great boobs, but I've got to ignore the cement mixer two inches to the south."

Suffice to say that having sex with your pregnant wife is not the ménage à trois you envisioned in your fantasies.

After the baby is born, you're completely shut out. She's even got a note from the doctor. Did you know that? Weeks, maybe months, with absolutely—Huh!—nothing! Given the choice of (a) a night of rapturous multiple-orgasmic sex and (b) a good night's sleep, sorry to say but there's no question she would choose (b). Which is okay with you. For one thing, you'd rather go play with the new toy than your old wife and, for another thing, the baby's presence will serve as a constant reminder of what can happen if you opt for plan (a).

You have to be kind to her now that you've gotten her into trouble. Now more than ever. No kidding around. She'll be a wreck. She'll have morning sickness and cravings and food aversions; she'll have to eat all the time and pee all the time. She'll be uncomfortable and won't sleep through the night and it's all your fault, you Penis man. You did this to her, Dr. Frankenstein, and now you have to shoulder the responsibility for your actions.

It's easy to be supportive, because you don't have to suffer any physical pain, and because now she holds all the cards. You will celebrate the forthcoming joyous event by catering to your wife's every whim for nine months. If you thought you used to get no respect, now you can add sympathy to the list of things you get none of. Even your friends will have a hard time siding with you in any disagreement over any issue, simply because she's pregnant. A friend was lamenting his pregnant wife's wild mood swings when I reminded him, "You are constantly being logical and rational." It almost never works with their breed, and especially not now. Even empathetic guys with kids can only offer you a knowing nod. They feel your pain, but they want you to know that they can't help you now, soldier. The advice they're likely to offer: "Duck!"

Being a pregnant couple almost certainly means taking some kind of class together, one in which you remind each other to breathe. You will meet other couples in this transient class and they will be your new friends. You need them. They may be the last new friends you ever make. These men know exactly what you're going through. They are just as freaked out as you are. You form a collective brotherhood of freaked-out men.

When you are collectively pregnant, one little thing will make the whole ordeal seem so much easier: Wait until the last possible moment to tell people. In our microwave world, nine months is an eternity. By the time you finally have the baby, people will be sick of it. They'll want to know what took you so long. If you can hold off till the four- or five-month marker, until she's "showing," you can successfully manage expectations—yours and theirs. Nine months should be enough time to prepare for anything, except this. You really don't know what you've gotten yourself into.

P.S.: Scientific evidence suggests that your dick isn't big enough to poke the baby's eye out. Billions of babies have been born, none with an eye poked out by Daddy's schlong.

CHILDREN

"I didn't make the same mistakes
my parents made when they raised me—
I was too busy making new ones."
—PAUL LANSKY

Children will be the most fulfilling and challenging experience of your life. They will make you a Family. They will make your life complete in ways you cannot even comprehend until it happens to you. The love you feel will be an entirely new sensation. A child will be the greatest source of pride, fear, joy, you name it. Any emotion you choose will be intensified in your feelings for your own flesh and blood. You will see the world through a child's eyes again, but with a lifetime of experience and wisdom. You will relive your own experiences and be treated to a changing world you would other-wise never know.

Yeah, fine.

Children will kill you. They are going to ruin your life. It's not the end of your life, but the end of your life as you knew it. They're going to suck up what's left of your time, suck all the money out of the treasury, and erase, once and for all, the thing you used to know as "space." Their arrival means that you are basically grounded for life. The kid is a standing date with a guilt trip. For the first time in your life you have some real impetus to set a good example, which means you can't drink and drive. You can't smoke or take drugs in front of the children. You can't listen to loud music or drink straight from the carton. In short, having a child around the house is like having your parents move in with you.

Don't allow yourself to be convinced by some dopey, politically correct child psychologist that if you buy a sword for your infant son you are encouraging violent antisocial behavior which will exhibit itself later as a murder spree down at the post office. These same dingalings say that if you get him a doll instead, it will lead the impressionable young man directly to the chorus line of a Rodgers and Hammerstein revival. The joke is that kids do whatever they want no matter what you do, show, ask, or tell them to do, often in direct contradiction to whatever you had in mind. So get him an Uzi or a Barbie dream house; it doesn't make a damn bit of difference. All roads lead to therapy, so why worry about it?

If you are lucky enough to have a baby girl, the thought going through your mind from birth to your own death is that she will meet guys like you someday. Every young man who comes a-calling at the door will be seen as having one central thought: the complete and total sexual degradation of Daddy's little girl. You will grudgingly become very, very polite with these lads, because you know that at the end of the day, one of them is going to marry her, get her off your balance sheet, and then she's his problem. In a roundabout way you need those boys. This is how karma works.

There is no winning with kids. If you don't give them what they want they will grow up deprived and callous, bitter and disappointed. If you do give them what they want they will be spoiled and insensitive to the needs of others, emotionally barren. Whatever you give them, they want something else. You can give them tennis lessons, but they'll want to play football. Take them skiing and soon it will come back to haunt you in the form of the three most dangerous words in the English language: "Follow me, Dad."

Babies are the greatest thing in the world, but you must know that they are utterly helpless and, if you put your emotional attachment aside, almost completely worthless. They don't do a damn thing for you. Human infants are the most helpless mammals on the planet. Baby zebras come out and run with the herd. Your children won't carry heavy bags to the airport until they're old enough to go away to school. They force you to watch Barney, the cancerous talking eggplant. They always need new clothes. They want every toy in the store. They are always hungry, and could live on food that would kill you in a matter of days. The only thing they ever clean up is a mess they made, and only rarely then. They don't cook or drive or earn money. They are an endless drain on the cash machine that you become over the course of their lives. They repay your endless devotion and bottomless love with statements like (Boy) "I'm taking the car," or (Girl) "I'm having his baby." Keep in mind that this is the reward awaiting you as you change Junior's diapers.

Children may be the light of your life, but in the day-to-day they will drive you to the brink of madness. Children make everything a struggle: getting in the car, talking on the phone, eating out, eating in, shopping, sleeping, fucking, you name it. There should be a "degree of difficulty" associated with various everyday tasks like there is with diving events in the Olympics.

They are cranky. They cry all the time. They can't be left alone for a minute. And if you thought your wife was always hanging around, a kid is a ball and chain for your other (i.e., the good) leg.

You will only be alone in the shower. Even then you're not safe. They come right in, totally oblivious to the fact that you're trying to hide from them. You can't tell them to go away. They have nowhere to go. Your rudest, most obnoxious friend will appear to be Prince Philip when compared to your own child.

Women have been preparing for this moment their whole lives. They played with dolls while you played with balls. They combed their hair, bathed them, dressed them, wheeled them around in a miniature baby carriage. You threw things and hit things. You'll be very helpful if the baby needs to be carried on a draw play or is suddenly hit to third base. You will look at that fragile bundle of your own flesh and blood thinking you're going to break it. Fear not, kids are very resilient. It is much harder to break one than you might think.

You'll want your friends to share in your excitement, to feel your joy, to experience the magic of this wonderful new force in your life. They're really, really, really happy for you—just not even close to as happy as you are. They can stomach about an hour of this happiness at a time unless they've got a little one of their own, in which case it doesn't matter. Which is just as well, because we probably don't want to see a whole huge group of people applauding the color of your baby's poo. It's just not the direction I want to see mankind go.

As soon as the baby pops out, both sides will start searching for relatives it looks like. If you're related to Winston Churchill or Lyndon Johnson, that's the end of the discussion. Otherwise, there's usually an Uncle Sidney who your two-month-old little girl resembles. Keep in mind that people make these same kinds of familial comparisons with adopted children, too. I'm sure the families of those babies who were switched at birth had some rethinking to do when they found out that their girls looked like someone else's Uncle Sidney.

Going to see the baby is one of the most bullshit events you'll ever attend. Men, by and large, don't gush and coo over little babies. I have a hard time saying much of anything at all. No matter what the thing looks like you're going to say something nice. You have to. Maybe you'll hold the baby for a couple minutes, but then what? Then somebody else holds the baby, that's what. The baby is like a baton in an incredibly slow, badly organized relay race.

For most of your friends, your baby means that they have to buy an impossibly small gift with an improbably big price tag, especially considering that the thing is going to be used up, thrown away, and forgotten about the time the check for the Visa bill clears their account. Some of these people already attended the engagement party, the bridal shower, the wedding, and the baby shower, and are looking at this last little trinket as the final installment payment in your friendship for quite a while. Pretty soon it will be their turn to bat and you'll be handing over more of the same crap to them.

Children develop at different rates. Men approach this like they were responsible for their baby passing any number of developmental hurdles: sleeping through the night, sitting up, crawling, talking, etc. Part of this is simply a healthy sense of paternal pride, but when was the last time you met a teenager in diapers who couldn't walk or read? No matter how much you try to help, or how badly you think you've messed up, they usually can do most of these things with a reasonable level of competence by the time the senior prom rolls around.

The real miracle is that anyone ever decides to have a second child. You'd think their curiosity would have been satisfied by one.

The rule of thumb is that if you have two, you might as well have five. Ask anyone with two. (Do not ask anyone who has five. They don't think it's funny anymore.) More often than not the intent is to give your child someone to play with as he or she grows up. Usually what winds up happening is that you've given them someone to torture and someone to conspire with against you in your declining years.

Naming a baby is one of the hardest things in the world. It's like picking a pair of sunglasses. You try on every pair in the store, even ones you know don't really suit your face, and then you whittle the choice down to just a few, and finally one emerges as the winner. No matter how happy you are with the pair that you ultimately settle on, there's always a little buyer's remorse. The first runner-up was good, too, maybe you should have tried on another pair. You yourself were thus named. It's a miracle more children aren't called Ray-Ban.

HER PLUMBING

"No man should marry until he has studied anatomy
and dissected at least one woman."
—HONORÉ DE BALZAC

In theory, the birth of your child is the most glorious moment of your life. In reality, childbirth is completely disgusting. Remember the famous scene from *Alien* where the creature crawls out of the guy's stomach? Imagine that scene in excruciatingly slow motion, under garishly bright lights, without music. You're beginning to get the picture.

Human reproduction is the natural order of things. Having a child is about as orderly as a hurricane. You will learn so much about the female anatomy, you'll be amazed. You'll be horrified. There is much more information than you ever wanted to know. All that fun stuff is incredibly complicated and, unlikely as this may have seemed when you first met, extremely functional. The more you know about them, the more impressive and frightening women become. These women are like some kind of industrial plumbing plant with about a million parts that all sound like you should whisper their names.

And of course we don't really want to know what they're going through. We don't want to pull a bowling ball out of our penises, we don't want to gain forty pounds in order to usher a completely helpless mammal into the world. There's so much stuff about continuing the family name that we don't want to deal with, it probably is worthwhile just to sign everything (your remaining 49 percent) over to her as soon as she "gets herself into trouble."

When you have your first child you will want to scream it from the rooftops. You will pass out cigars to your friends, carry pictures in your wallet, and tell strangers in line at the store about your good fortune. You will invite people over to see the miracle baby, but your friends will probably be more interested in seeing your wife's suddenly, implausibly huge, gigantic miracle tits. Most have never seen nipples as big as pancakes before, and will take an unusually scientific curiosity in their approach to the whole matter of breast-feeding, especially considering that these are the same guys who used to ditch biology class with you back in high school.

These pioneering scientists (boobologists) will not be able to look the mother of your child in the eye when Junior gets hungry and goes to work on one of those milk balloons. They'll sneak a peek, but only the womenfolk actually have the stomach to sit and watch the lactating process (or maybe it's just that they're the only ones who can say something like "isn't that sweet" without the generous hint of snickering irony you bring to it). When you witness this wonderful, apparently innocent scene, keep in mind the English proverb that "Children suck the mother when they are young and the father when they are old."

Your wife and mother of your child will now have to retrofit the baby factory and convert it into a dairy farm. They're very versatile, these women. You will soon find that there is a lot to know about breast-feeding. Books, seminars, videos, you name it. More than you thought was possible to know about the most basic female human activity after childbirth itself. I mean, illiterate Central American Indians knock out a kid a year, stick out a functioning mammary gland, and go on about their business grinding corn or beating clothes on a rock or whatever the hell it is they do. Simple enough. It doesn't involve a trip in the Volvo to Barnes & Noble. When the baby cries, there's a 75 percent chance that it's hungry. FEED IT. Women throughout time and all over the world have managed this without a lot of hubbub.

You will have to choose whether or not to taste the breast milk straight from the tap. By the way, fellas, this is what those round mounds of fatty tissue are for: making milk. The little pencil erasers at the end are where the milk comes out, did you know that? Some men just can't handle it. They'd rather eat a bug than taste mother's milk straight from the source. Others (myself included) can't wait to get in there, but ultimately wind up a bit disappointed that the stuff inside isn't nearly as much fun as the container it comes in.

There is a device you should know about called a breast pump. It is basically an Acu-Jac to get the milk out of the mother and into a bottle for more convenient feeding later. This completes the transition from "hot piece of ass" to agricultural processing/exporting plant, all of which began when you made the decision to get into the animal husbandry business. When Bob's wife got one of these contraptions, he took away her charge cards and high-heel shoes and started calling her "Bessie." That didn't go over too well.

BECOMING YOUR PARENTS

"**Parents:** A peculiar group who first try to get their children to walk and talk, and then try to get them to sit down and shut up."

—WAGSTER'S DICTIONARY OF HUMOR AND WIT

What a difference a day makes. You are now proud parents of a little baby. It's like getting a new job, a new wife, and a new video game all on the same day you're having a dinner party. It becomes immediately apparent that there really should have been some sort of entrance exam to get into this line of work.

The joyous addition to your life (the yin, if you will) has another side to it (the yang): the complete loss of conversational skills for the next several years, possibly the rest of your natural life. You will not be able to sustain a conversation for fifteen minutes without some direct or indirect reference to children. You're like an agent with only one client. In his very funny book *Fatherhood*, Bill Cosby says, "My wife and I often summoned the grandparents of our first baby and proudly cried, 'Look! Poopoo!' A statement like this is the greatest single disproof of evolution I know." By the time Junior is old enough to talk, you may have nothing worthwhile to say to him.

If your friends beat you to the punch and have children before you do, you will find that they become unbelievably boorish, one-dimensional, and selfish because all they can talk about is their kid.

If, on the other hand, you get there first, you will find that your friends have become unbelievably boorish, one-dimensional, and selfish, because they don't want to talk only about your kid.

I'm sure you'll be disappointed when you realize that you're not a rebel or a revolutionary or a punk anymore. Okay, so you're a sellout sucker like every other schnook out there making a living with a wife and a kid and a mortgage and a sore knee. Ha! That was a quick and reasonably painless transition. All that youthful idealism, the romantic, socialistic, utopian notions you espoused so eloquently in your college philosophy thesis, seems to belong to someone you used to know. The more you protest, the more true, painful, and harder the fall to the rank of schnook-like-every-body-else will be. Don't take your hair or your health too lightly, amigo, they're next.

Being a parent is like being Judge Judy on speed. You're adjudicating seven hundred misdemeanors and civil actions every day. "Guilty—put that down!" "Motion carried—you can watch a video during dinner." "Conviction overturned on appeal—you can eat that." All day, every day. Court opens at 7:00 A.M. and it never closes. My sister, in one run-on sentence, said: "Christopher, please sit down, eat your dinner, you don't have to yell." Judy, Judy, Judy.

Being a parent will make you brave beyond your imagination. Nothing disgusts you anymore. If you wipe somebody else's tushy every day for a couple years you have to be made of tough stuff. We should send armies of parents into battle, nobody would fuck with them.

You will assume several other functions, none of which are discussed in any of the parenting books I read. Specifically, you are now a bodyguard, staff photographer, historian, pediatrician, and a god.

The bodyguard gig comes naturally. Your basic, primal instinct for self-protection is heightened when your child is involved. A walk in the park with a stroller is like being with the Secret Service following the President into a crowd. Everyone looks suspicious, especially if they're on wheels or involved with flying objects.

As staff photographer, no nuance of your infant child's life will go unnoticed by the camera. After my nephew was born the guy at the Fotomat asked my father with amazement, "So many pictures and only one child?" This phenomenon parallels the Big Bang theory of the birth of the universe; the level and intensity of activity dissipates in direct correlation with the age of the child. There are fewer new pictures of my six-and-a-half-year-old nephew. In my mother's menagerie of family photos there is only one picture of me since high school. Fortunately, you don't have to be any good as a photographer to play at being Hurrell. You buy a lot of expensive  equipment to make it look like you know what you're doing, and the rest of your family will tell you when and where and how to chronicle Junior's early development, you fucking idiot.

You are now a god. Not God, but a god. For the first years they are yours to play with as you see fit. As proof of your new standing in the pantheon, now you're an Authority on Everything. Especially all the unknowable things. Your wife also knows everything there is to know about everything; unfortunately she's got an outdated copy of the manual. There's always 10 percent down the line who never get the word, and you're sure she falls into that group when you get into a dispute. Eventually, the child gets wise that you're not perfect and then the god party is over. Usually that happens when they learn to say the word "no."

It is only fitting that you begin to act the part of "parent" but—and this is a big but—the real wake-up call about children has nothing to do with them. It has to do with the moment when you hear yourself channeling your mother's voice telling your child to "Go to your room" or "No dessert for you" or words to that effect. Remember, not long ago, one of the millions of times when you promised yourself that this wasn't going to happen to you? That you were going to be different? Well, ha! That was a good one. The joke's on you, buddy. Congratulations, you have become not just parents, but you are now your own parents.

In fact, you may recall your parents putting the curse on you: "I hope you have children just like you someday." Well, now what are you gonna do? Your frustration and disappointment is their vengeful glee. Man makes plans, God laughs.

The Talmud says that "when a young man marries, he divorces his mother." Or so you thought. One day you will awaken to the eerie Kafkaesque awareness that your wife is becoming not just a mother, but your mother. You knew that she was going to become more like her mother, but this is the kind of thing that makes you wake up in a cold sweat. If given a choice, you'd probably rather have her evolve into a cockroach. One friend recently told me: "I love my mother, don't get me wrong, but I didn't get married so I could spend more time with her."

My friend Drew says that there is exactly one woman. One wife, one mother, one woman. Tell any guy a story about your scary mother or wife, he can beat it. I know, for example, that I'll go to visit my mother in the home when she's ninety, I'll be sixty-five, my sister will be sixty-four. I'll put down the flowers we brought, give her a kiss hello, but her furrowed brow will immediately tell me that something's not right. "What's the matter, Ma?"

"How could you wear those socks with that suit?"

I told this story, a little joke to illustrate my relationship with my mother, to a woman I was dating, a divorcée named Joni who has a six-year-old son. She said, "I do that." Joni is a psychiatrist. There is no help for any of us.

KEEPING SCORE

As men, we are goal oriented. We like sports because there are winners and losers, goal lines to cross, scores we can tabulate, tangible minutiae we can read meaning into. We like gambling for the same reasons. You know exactly where you stand. Gloria Steinem says "the reason most women don't gamble is that their total instinct for gambling is satisfied by marriage."

Your marriage is probably the most important thing in your life. You love the Bulls, but not like this. You wouldn't take a bullet for Toni Kukoc. So why aren't there any statistics for you to keep track of your marriage? You can't just look in the paper and see where you rank, like the weather report. It could be very helpful in practical ways: "Maybe I should wear a coat. Maybe I should give her a foot massage." There ought to be a points-rebounds-assists kind of spread for you to check every day. You may be ahead of someone who's having an affair. Maybe and maybe not. Without a point spread you'll never know.

There are couples who fight like cats and dogs. You don't know how they make it from one day to the next. You'd be looking for new lodgings if you had that particular fight with your wife, but they like it that way. Somehow they keep on going and going like the Energizer bunny. Would you say they're connecting on 50 percent of their attempts?

Your wife may help you negotiate this difficult question, and maybe not. If you ask her how she is and she says "I'm fine," that could mean that she's fine, not to worry, everything's cool. It may also mean anything else in the color spectrum, including "I'm not fine, and I'm not telling you exactly how not fine I am. Yet."

We need structure, an ongoing reminder of where we are and what's happening, a scorecard or a scoreboard. There ought to be something like an exit poll in which every day you and your wife are asked a handful of questions; what are the issues and what is your position? If you think it's going badly, you're right. She thinks so, too. You may be the last to know. She thought so before it even occurred to you and has talked about it with almost everyone she knows. Just ask her. She's been waiting for you to ask her. For a divorce.

Marriage is counterintuitive to men. We like football because it's so precise. Fifteen-minute quarters. The game is over and somebody wins. If not, you have sudden death overtime. Marriage isn't about winning. You never win anything. Marriage is about muddling through to another anniversary. You win by not losing. The game never ends. The goal is just to keep playing together nicely. Marriage is about intangibles. Poor ugly people can be happy while rich beautiful people are unhappy. Richard Gere and Cindy Crawford got a divorce. It makes no sense whatsoever.

CHEATING

"Live dangerously carefully."
—ARMAND HAMMER

After a man is married he has the legal right to deceive only one woman. There is nothing stopping you from cheating on your wife. You can do anything you want, it's totally open. You can yell "Fire!" in a crowded theater; tug on Superman's cape; pee on a cop car; ski off a cliff; pick a fight with a bouncer. There are a lot of exciting, dangerous, stupid things you can do.

Cheating on your wife is incredibly easy to do. Men do it all the time. It's the oldest trick in the book. It's one of the Ten Commandments that Charlton Heston brought down from the mountain, somewhere between "Thou shalt not kill" and "Thou shalt not do the *New York Times* crossword puzzle in ink." You probably won't get caught unless you want to—and Dr. Freud might suggest that if you are cheating on your wife, somehow you do want to—get caught.

Not that it's always the completely wrong thing to do. *Newsweek* published a poll that said about 22 percent of those questioned thought an affair could sometimes be good for a marriage. Yes, but only if it's already completely fucked up. Like a heart attack can be just the thing to improve your diet. For the record, we here at the *Life Sentence* Institute strongly suggest that you don't cheat on your wife until you have exhausted all other resources.

A friend named Charlie married a model. He was that kind of guy. I could not believe it when I heard he was running around on her. In my simplistic worldview, I wondered: Who do you cheat with if you've got a 10 at home? The answer is "strange." You just want something different. Why, Charlie? Because we're fucking idiots. Even foie gras and sauterne gets to be boring if you have it every night. "Show me a 3 and I can make her a 10," said another married guy with a foxy wife about any woman who wasn't already his foxy wife. We can't help it. If you've got a brunette, you want a blonde and vice versa. Bad dog.

Some guys cheat on their wives with married women. What are they thinking? Someone should take them aside and say, "You've already got one wife too many, man." As a kid, you may have wanted to live with one of your friends' families. They seemed to be so much cooler than your own parents, but now they look like the Addams Family. So it is with your married mistress. If you had to actually keep her (it almost never comes to this, but if it did) you'd have second thoughts (and so should she), especially considering her very liberal take on the fidelity issue.

This next bit should already be known to every man alive. I should not have to put ink to paper, but I may save a marriage down the line, so here goes: If you visit a prostitute, do not give her your phone number, do not tell her where you live, do not tell her where you work. Do not give her your real name. Be anyone you want to be, except yourself. Make it up. Tell her your name is Clark Kent and you're a mild-mannered reporter for the *Daily Planet*—she doesn't give a shit who you are as long as you pay with cash money up front. Don't say anything that could come back to you. This happened to a guy we know and it was so bad you would have a hard time imagining how bad. (Okay, it was funny because the guy is such a schmuck, but it was really bad.) Even his lawyer said, "You gave a hooker your phone number? *This* is bad."

Seriously: If you are going to cheat on your wife, wear a condom. You hate condoms. I hate condoms. Everyone hates condoms. Condoms are the enemy of everything we love. Condoms are the worst thing in the world. Except for one thing: giving your wife a dose of something bad. Hell hath no fury like a woman infected with a sexually transmitted disease by her cheating husband. Getting dosed is worse than getting Mickeyed, maced, or rolled. Try to imagine how this is going to sound in court, which is where it will end up if you're too stupid not to wear a condom. Further, harking back to the days of yesteryear, when we wore condoms because we didn't want to knock up our high school sweetheart, it's going to be a world of hurt when your mistress files a paternity suit. If you can't keep Jimmy in your pants, put a hat on him.

One thing to keep in mind at all times, stud: Tell no one. Absolutely no one. Don't tell your best friend. Don't tell an old friend. Don't tell any living person who does not have a professional ethical reason to not tell anyone else. This is not information that is on a "need to know" basis. This is the real "I'd tell you but I'd have to kill you" information. Top secret. The stuff of which hot gossip is made, and your life hangs precipitously in the balance. People love to share this stuff, they cannot resist the impulse to do so, and thus the responsibility falls to you. If you really need to let it out, tell your priest, your shrink, your lawyer or doctor. And don't take any chances: Swear them to secrecy before you say a word. If you wouldn't trust them with your life, you can't trust them to shut the hell up about this.

Of all the people you know who have had affairs, how did you find out about most of them? Did they confide in you personally or did you hear it from someone they confided in personally? Or someone a little further down the line? Right. Secrets have a way of mushrooming and taking on a life of their own. (The Mathematical Rule of Gossip is this: Take the number of people that you know who know about something and square it to get the actual number of people who know.) Make no mistake, a secret is impossible to get back into the bottle once it's out.

If anyone, especially your wife, asks you about your affair, follow the Richard Pryor Principle and deny it. If they have pictures, deny it. If they catch you in flagrante delicto, deny it. Tell bold-faced lies. Tell them they're crazy, they're reading too much into it, they're imagining things, they don't know what they're talking about. "Who are you going to believe, me or your lying eyes?"

Cheating is about more than sex, of course. Intimacy is the thing that most people go looking for outside their marriage, something they're not getting at home. A woman told me the reason she was having an affair was that her husband didn't scratch her back. Scratch her back, husband, and cover your own. If you want something special, ask your wife for it first. They love talking about all that relationship crap. If she doesn't get with the program, at least you asked.

Of course cheating is more fun than having sex with your wife, but nobody ever said anything about marriage being fun. You have no responsibility to your mistress. Marilyn Monroe once said, "Husbands are chiefly good as lovers when they are betraying their wives." An affair involves a lot of planning, like a small but vitally important military operation. There are dozens of decisions to make: determining when and where to meet for a discreet rendezvous, establishing a slush fund for covert cash payments, hushed phone calls creating plausible alibis, constantly looking over your shoulder to see who's following you. Maintaining intimate secrets is cloak-and-dagger stuff, a high-stakes game with very serious consequences if you should be discovered behind enemy lines.

There is a pretty good chance that your wife will want to kill you if she catches you, so be very, very careful. Be discreet, if not valorous, but don't wear a disguise. You'll have more trouble trying to explain the fake mustache than what you were doing in the wrong place with a strange woman in the first place, and your wife will recognize you anyway.

Even if you want to get caught.

DIVORCE

"Bigamy is having one wife too many.
Monogamy is the same."

—OSCAR WILDE

The marriage contract specifically states: "Forever, until death do you part." There is no way that anyone would sign off on that deal for anything else. Except in the Mob. Only the Mafia offers the same terms, and they have only a marginally more threatening means of arbitration: You want out, there's the witness protection program or you sleep with the fishes—either of which will seem like a holiday in Tahiti compared to a divorce. Divorce is just like death, an out clause, only you can take half of it with you when you go. (You will recall that she owns 51 percent of everything, so if you get anything at all it's only because she doesn't want it anymore.)

Divorce is just a fight that didn't go the distance. There is no social stigma attached to it. Getting a divorce is so easy nowadays you shouldn't hesitate about getting married. Choosing when to finally throw in the towel is like trying to decide when to yank the starting pitcher. Would you rather see if he can battle it out for another inning, maybe find his stride after a rocky start; or do you pull the plug before it really gets ugly? You're either too early or too late, no matter what. Nobody ever got a divorce at the ideal moment.

Not likely to be next in the series of Old Milwaukee "wouldn't it be great if . . ." beer ads: Wouldn't it be great if your wife knew when it was time to end it and just said "it was great fun, but it was just one of those things . . . I understand . . . no hard feelings . . . I'll get my stuff later . . . call me if you just want to talk or maybe get it on sometime, okay? I'll be fine. Bye." Yeah, right. And then she turned into a six-pack and a hot pizza.

Still, for a lot of people in bad situations, signing the final divorce papers can be the happiest moment of the marriage since she tossed the bouquet. And the good news with a divorce is that you also get rid of your mother-in-law.

Clark Gable once said that the reason he frequented prostitutes was because he could pay them to go away. Divorce is the end result of a similar cost-benefit analysis. Your obligation may depend on your level of investment in the deal, and buying your way out of a bad marriage may seem like a steal at any price. In ancient Rome, slaves could buy their freedom, and so can you. What's it worth? You'll find out. It may be cheaper to keep her.

Before you get a divorce you'll probably get separated. A trial separation. The question you have to face during a trial separation is whether you're trying to get back together, or you're practicing being single again. Harvey says that no one ever gets "separated." By that he means that everyone who does ultimately gets divorced. The statistics are in his favor. "The difference between legal separation and divorce is that a legal separation gives a husband time to hide his money," said Johnny Carson. He learned that one the hard way.

Divorce is an example of female vampirism in contemporary society. You may not have married a gold-digging ball buster, but that's what you'll be looking at across the table in court. She and her barracuda are going to try to take you for everything you've got, but your peace of mind has a certain value (a complex ratio of money and emotions), and you will determine what it's worth to get rid of her on your own personal "misery index." Norman Mailer said, "You don't know anything about a woman until you meet her in court."

If there are no kids from the marriage, it was basically a well-publicized bad date. It's a breakup with a girlfriend, except that people feel you owe them something back in exchange for the wedding gift. Oops, you goofed, but at least you've got six (of twelve) place settings to show for it. Which now makes your choice of number two doubly important. Most everyone is willing to spot you one little mistake, but don't let it happen again. If you blow your second chance you're a real loser.

Be very, very sure about your divorce. I know a guy who left his wife for "the other woman" he was having an affair with. He told his wife that the girlfriend was not as good looking, was not as good a cook, but "she loves sex" (by which he meant to say that she swallows). The guy goes away on an organized camping trip to Alaska and wakes up one night to find the girlfriend in some other guy's sleeping bag. Meanwhile, his estranged wife meets a guy who sets her off like a string of firecrackers on Chinese New Year. This guy who left his family to be a stud found out, too late, that both his wife and his girlfriend love sex, just with other guys. His ex-wife got the house, the car, alimony, custody, and child support. And, as a bonus, a younger man who really rocks her world. He, in turn, got a one-bedroom apartment, half the CD collection, some camping gear, and an ex-girlfriend. That's gotta hurt. Now the poor schmuck is on his knees begging her to take him back. "I'll be good. I'll change." Yeah. He has already shown her his capacity for change: He went from Husband to Adulterer to Divorcé to Sniveling Whining Loser. Where can he possibly go from here?

When a guy leaves his wife for another *guy*, he's probably very, very sure.

This is known as the "trigger effect" of a divorce. You undoubtedly imagined that things would be better for you once you lost 110 pounds, but whenever reality intrudes on fantasy there is bound to be some bitter disappointment.

Of course, there is the outside chance that she leaves you. At the outset, you didn't even consider this possibility, did you? Your little angel wouldn't be out whoring around with half the town. Would you rather have her leave you (a) because she simply can't stand you and would rather be alone? (b) for another man? or (c) for another woman?

With (a) you probably feel the same way. With (b) you have to wonder "what does he have that I don't have?" At least with another woman, you can't really compete, so you're not looking over your shoulder for the rest of your life wondering "what does she have that I don't have?" It's obvious. Instead, Gender-Bender, you'll be wondering what

you did to drive her there. It wasn't you. It was, as they say over at the Pleasure Chest, "preference."

If a man steals your wife, conventional wisdom says that there is no better revenge than to let him keep her.

If you made a mistake, get out of it as soon as possible. Rob married Sheryl in college and always hated her. To be fair, her domineering personality pushed him to become a wealthy man. Their first joint tax return out of college was for $9,000. She relentlessly prodded him to become a success as a writer and producer in television, almost despite himself, but he was sick of her long before any of that happened. Then along came two kids and he was too busy to notice how miserable he'd become. (He was a miserable sod to begin with, but that's not the point of this story.) It wasn't until he'd sold his show into syndication that he started running around and finally asked for a divorce. Except that his last joint tax return was for $36 million. Timing is everything, and the ultimate "fuck you" is to make a huge score the day *after* the papers come through.

You've got to love Catholics. They can't get divorced and stay in the Church (remember all that Henry VIII stuff?), so they've worked it out in a way that, thank God, is not cynical or hypocritical whatsoever. They simply get an annulment. This is the deal you used to hear about when somebody woke up in Tijuana with a tequila hangover and a surprise lying in bed next to him with a wedding license in her purse. Or maybe the parents got wise to their teenage daughter's elopement a day late and put an end to it quickly. They just cancel the contract. Fine. Just a big misunderstanding, let's part company, don't want any problems, I wish you well on your future endeavors. My friend Lisa is one of five children ages twenty-five to thirty-five. Her parents got an annulment. All they had to do was swear that they never loved each other in the course of their thirty-eight-year marriage, pay a small stipend to the right lawyer and a little something to the parish. Then someone in a funny hat blessed the event, sprinkled some holy water around, mumbled something in Latin, crossed himself and said, "If you want to get married again it's okay with us." That wacky Pope, he's got all the angles covered. (Then they had to get a state-sanctioned divorce to make it legal.) I, for one, am happy to know that there's no hypocrisy in the Church.

SINGLE AGAIN

"Marrying an old bachelor is like
buying second-hand furniture."
—HELEN ROWLAND

The good news is, fellas, that you stand to benefit enormously from this sea change. After you get over the sticker shock of what it costs to be a free man, and what "the lifestyle she's become accustomed to" really means, you'll be an eligible bachelor all over again. Do not mourn the death of your marriage. It is a mistake to think that there is nothing so bad about a breakup that a cheap, drunken, meaningless roll in the hay won't fix, but it couldn't hurt. Let the restorative powers of sex with a virtual stranger wash over you and help you rise out of your funk.

You are alone for the first time in a while, and all you can think about is getting together with someone else as soon as possible. If you were thinking ahead, you would have already lined up your next deal. If not, you start again from scratch. You're coming out of retirement. Michael Jordan did it, you can, too. Dating again is just like riding a horse after you've been thrown; you've got to get right back up and seduce another horse.

After you get divorced you will befriend other divorced guys. Married guys either don't want to be seen with you, as if you were contagious, or, worse, they want to help you. As part of your healing process you may want to join a men's support group, a form of group therapy where you and those like you gather to bash women in a nonjudgmental communal environment. It's good to know that you're not alone—there are a lot of bitter, vitriolic men who can help you get through the rough spots.

You will be a far more eligible bachelor now than at any time when you were originally single. You've already shown that you're the marrying type, and women can almost smell the weird mix of yearning, desperation, and pent-up sexual energy. Now you have a certain enigmatic sadness they can't resist, a heart on your sleeve. If you grow a goatee and buy a midlife crisis convertible, you've got it all. They will be drawn to you like moths to cashmere; you have Ex appeal where there was once Sex appeal.

You will go out to bars and clubs and restaurants, discover a whole new world you never knew existed while you were married. "You mean this has been here all this time? Why didn't anybody tell me? I should've done this years ago!"

Half or more of the women you meet now are divorcées, and one way or another they're almost all damaged goods. They're in the same boat as you, except they get the check instead of having to write it. If only you could get a woman who continued to receive her alimony after you married her, like a songwriter's copyrights. An annuity. But, alas, no. The government never gives you a break like that.

Divorced women all want to talk about it. They want to get into their therapy with you. She'll want to open up to you about what a rat bastard her ex-husband was. What an insensitive jerk he was and all the shitty stuff he did to her. You probably don't want to hear about it. In fact, most of it sounds vaguely familiar. Part of your penance for being a divorced guy is that now you have to suffer through when some other guy's ex-wife starts ranting about some bullshit. If you're smart you'll take her side. "Oh yeah, that's terrible. I agree." You may come away from a date feeling like you should send her a bill for $150 for the session.

The good thing about a divorce is that you really do get a "do over." You can start from square one, remake your life. You can also fuck some of your old girlfriends, which you couldn't do when you were married. That's two good things. Of course, if this was a bitter disentanglement, if you really were the wounded one, you might want to bone one or more of her gal pals. Women, being incredibly duplicitous, such as they are, will have no problem dissing your ex while they're sleeping with you. Your ex will find out and, really, what better way is there to say "fuck you"? Besides, what is she going to do, fire you? I don't think so.

YOUR
SECOND WIFE

"One wife is as good as another,
if not better."

Nobody ever went into a marriage and hoped it would end in a divorce. No man, anyway. (There may be a few women who married solely with the intention of improving their social standing after a divorce.) According to Helen Rowland, "When you see what some girls marry, you realize how they must hate to work for a living." Nobody said "I hope this turns into a train wreck," but it happens all the time. Swing and a miss. Nothing to be ashamed of. All good things must come to an end and, thankfully, so shall this piece of shit marriage you wound up in.

The rules are somewhat different for the second wife, however. Remember how you couldn't talk about your ex-girlfriends to your wife? Your ex-wife is now the evil thing in the closet. You may only refer to her in a negative way. You may never defend her, no matter what your leftover feelings about her may be, if your new wife is the one doing the analysis. You see, you've been down a lot of these roads before. If you had children in your first marriage, having a child with the new wife is like a fireman going to put out a blaze. Your adrenaline gets going, there's a lot of commotion, but it's just part of the job for you, another day at the office. Although you can never admit this or say things like, "When Melissa was born . . ."

You're under no real obligation to stay married to the second wife. You've already said "till death" once and you haven't been stricken down yet. Look how you spit in God's face with the first one. Ha! Spending eternity in the kingdom of heaven is looking less and less like a sure thing, but you don't have to live with your ex-wife anymore, so we'll call it a push.

Some guys are like marriage junkies. I sometimes get the feeling they confused their vows with the directions on the side of the shampoo bottle: "Marry. Divorce. Repeat if desired." Who, in their right mind, having been divorced, desires to get married a second time?

Some guys marry the same kind of woman over and over, they have a "type." They're like addicts, they can't help themselves. Some guys even remarry the same woman. The exact same woman. What the fuck is that all about? Liz and Dick did it. Did something happen that made them think it would be different the next time? Was it Sinatra singing "Love's more comfortable the second time around"? Did they just forget what it was like during the filming of *Cleopatra*?

It may just be that you married the wrong woman the first time. The second marriage often works out precisely because you figured out what you don't want in a wife and partner and what you really can't stand in another living person—the things that drive you to the brink of homicidal behavior. This is known in lay terms as Plan B. At least it's a fresh starting point. Hopefully, you'll get it right on the second pass.

So off you go a second time. You freely undertake to remarry knowing full well what lies ahead. There is no sucker punch in a second marriage, but if it doesn't work out you have to start admitting to yourself that this just isn't your gig. Your friends are sick of buying wedding gifts for you. After your first marriage and divorce (now referred to as "the cluster fuck"), they're going to wait the full twelve-month grace period before they charge another setting of Waterford. By the third wedding they'll just get you a lottery ticket and wish you luck. By the third wedding you won't be wearing a tuxedo, you'll be wearing a rabbit's foot. Skip it. You're not cut out for this line of work. You might gain some kind of arcane wisdom from the experience, like Peter deVries, who said: "I don't for the life of me understand why people keep insisting marriage is doomed. All five of mine worked out."

A very funny woman named Helen Rowland said, "A bride at her second marriage does not wear a veil. She wants to see what she is getting." So should you. If you do decide to marry a divorcée, go have lunch with her ex-husband, and try to keep from laughing when the "till death do you part" stuff comes up.

AGING

"A man finds himself seven years older
the day after his marriage."
—FRANCIS BACON

You're going to get older faster. No one can stop the march of time, but marriage will age a man faster than the absence thereof. Have you noticed that single and/or divorced guys all look tan and fit? They have to be. You don't. They're getting ready for something. They're in the hunt. They're possibly trying to impress somebody. They swagger when they walk. Married guys walk like they're going up a hill.

A woman can go either way after she gets married. The pressure is off so there is less anxiety, less stress, which means less wrinkles. She is confident in herself, secure in her relationship, and wants to keep herself in shape to keep her man happy. On the other hand, she knows that working to attract a man is a thing of the past, and may let herself go. (You don't see a lot of married broads over at the gym. Just going to the gym is an admission that you need to go to the gym.) This can happen very slowly or all at once. You must be very careful in dealing with your wife's appearance. If left unchecked, she could quietly gain five to seven pounds a year and wind up looking thirty pounds too much like her mother in less than five years.

Gloria Steinem says that "Women age, but men mature." This is one of the great unfairnesses of all time: As men get older they begin to look like Sean Connery. As women get older they begin to look like . . . Sean Connery.

On the other hand (this marriage business often takes more than two hands), if you keep the pressure on about her appearance (i.e., if you obsess about it as much as she already does), it will come back to you in ways and at moments you could never expect. It will be during the fourth quarter of the NFC Championship game, perhaps, that she will ask you "Does my ass look fat to you?" The answer "No!" should come as a reflex, not "Honey, this is neither the time nor the place, and would you please move your fat ass, I can't see the fucking TV."

Be prepared if she asks: "Would you still love me as much if I was fat?" On the surface, this seems to call for a yes or no answer. "No" is simply wrong wrong wrong, but "yes," which may shut her up (and lead her to the mistaken sense of security in the belief that you're not as shallow as you seem), also gives her license to dive head-first into a gallon of Häagen-Dazs and, eventually, wear a muumuu. Instead, give a qualified answer—i.e., "Yes, I would still love you as much if you were fat, but I would prefer, strictly for my own selfish, wrongheaded, male-ego reasons, that you were not fat." Qualified answers are one of the keys to a long and happy marriage.

Mel Brooks said, "We mock the things we are to be." You're going to become an old man, an *alter kocker*, a grandfather. What are you going to do? What choice do you have? As you get older your thinking will change. You won't feel a thing, but you may find yourself agreeing more with your parents. You'll see the wisdom in what they say and, as Dennis Miller points out, they ain't getting any hipper.

If you live long enough, you are going to become an old married couple. Considering the alternatives, it's nice to grow old with someone. In his very funny book *Couplehood*, Paul Reiser says: "When you've been together long enough, you know each other's stories. That's why a lot of times you see couples in their eighties sitting and not talking: They've heard everything. They Know. 'When we got married, I told you everything I had done up to that point. And since then, you were there. What could I possibly tell you?' "

If you finished each other's sentences when you were courting, it was because you were so excited, because it was cute to show how the two of you were of one mind. That novelty wears off quickly, though. By now it means that you've both heard all this crap before and are interrupting to (a) embellish with a very important point that the other was about to omit from the story, without which the meaning would be lost, or (b) omit the same trifling, pedantic detail that adds nothing to the story, mercifully speeding the process along for the unwitting listener. Cut to the punch line.

According to statistics—which are statistically inaccurate in all fields of human endeavor except sports—married men enjoy the best mental health of any group, while married women have the worst. As you get older you can be secure in the knowledge that the whole time you thought she was driving you crazy, it was quite the other way around.

Youth is wasted on the young, and with age comes wisdom. Milton Berle says that "The trouble is, by the time you can read a girl like a book, your library card has expired." You still like to look, but you don't necessarily know why. You become like an old dog who still likes to sniff around, but now it's more out of habit than curiosity or desire.

You go to a locker room somewhere and see some *alter kockers* wandering around with their balls halfway to their knees and you wonder—are they still doin' it? My dad's friend James says that after sixty you never want to waste a hard-on, no matter where you are or who you're with. You don't know when or where the next one is going to pop up, so make the most of it. Just looking at them, it can be a pretty frightening thought, but you see these guys shooting a 10-handicap or playing a decent game of tennis, and you start to think maybe they've got some Old Man wisdom now, some Zen thing where even if they don't get it up as often, they make every opportunity count. They play the finesse game, not power. They rely on experience and knowledge, not exuberance and experimentation. Old age and cunning will beat youth and speed every time.

As you get older you may come to care less about sex, with the concomitant rise in your level of interest in various other bodily functions. Given a choice between sex and a really good pee, it's no contest. You'll take the pee. Don't even get me started about number two. If you're over sixty-five and regular you'll wear it like a badge of honor, the Croix de Guerre. While others are schlepping to the drugstore for things that make you go, things that make you stop going, softeners and hardeners, you'll be dancing around the room singing "I feel pretty." A good dump can make you feel years younger, but getting laid just makes you tired.

Some of the chief pleasures of growing old together are watching your wife's hair turn from gray back to black, seeing her move into a stage of life where she becomes "handsome," and looking back at some of the people you didn't marry. Hopefully you will grow nearsighted together.

A friend's parents recently got a divorce after almost forty years together. This is happening a lot lately. Evidently, you suddenly wake up after twenty-five or thirty or forty years and say "I'm not happy. See ya." After a certain length of time, people should be forced to stay together. There is a joke about a couple in their late eighties who get a divorce after fifty-plus years of marriage. Here's the punch line: "We were waiting for the children to die."

The best part of getting older is becoming a grandparent. It doesn't upset your life in any negative way and, now that you can afford anything you want, nobody tries to sell you anything, so you can spoil the kid like mad. Grandparents and grandchildren have a special bond . . . because they have a common enemy.

DEATH

"When I said 'till death do us part,'
I never dreamt I'd live so long."
—POSTCARD

Joke: Guy goes to the doctor. The doctor says, "I've got bad news, you're going to die and there's nothing I can do." The guy goes home and tells his wife, then he says, "And I've got something to confess: I've been unfaithful to you several times over the years. Do you forgive me?" His wife says, "I forgive you ... but you better die."

There have been billions of people and not one has ever had a happy ending. The same can be said for marriages. If you manage to keep the music playing long enough, if you can avoid all the land mines in the road, there is only one guarantee: Somebody's gonna die first. Sorry, but nobody's getting out of this sucker alive. Death do you part.

Another joke: Mr. Levine dies in the arms of a young prostitute. Mrs. Levine goes to get a headstone made for her husband's grave site and tells the stone mason, "I want the stone to read: Rest in Peace, Until I Get There."

The gentlemanly thing to do is to observe "ladies first," which leaves you behind to handle things—and then remarry or die alone. A few months after my grandmother died, my grandfather went to join her. He had been sick for a while, but the conventional wisdom is that he died of a broken heart. This is a common denouement, and an unfortunate one because, if you've still got your marbles, you're now free to do whatever you want: take up smoking, get a tattoo, drink and gamble your money away. For the first time in a long time nobody's telling you what not to do. If you wind up in this situation, don't waste it.

Another joke: Guy goes to the doctor. The doctor says, "I've got bad news, you're going to die, and I only give you another twenty-four hours to live." The guy goes home and tells his wife. They have dinner at their favorite place, a great bottle of wine, and go home and make love. When they're done he wants to do it again. His wife says: "Easy for you to say, you don't have to get up in the morning."

There is this much consolation if she predeceases you: You don't have to worry about your lowlife friends moving in on your wealthy widow now that you are, sadly, out of the picture. These rat bastards won't wait until your body is cold before they start hustling her, and that very instinct is why they were your friends.

Joke: Why do Jewish men die before their wives do? Answer: Because they want to!

After you tend to the very unfortunate business of the funeral and its aftermath, you will be in demand like never before. It is a statistical fact that women outlive men by about seven years, so if you find yourself suddenly single, you're in the driver's seat, Grandpa.

Something called the "Brisket Brigade" will visit itself upon you in the personage of eligible little old ladies who show up under the guise of "concern" for you now that you are "alone." These widows and divorcées will bring you something to eat, perhaps a little something they made in order to showcase their prowess in at least one room of the house. They will be throwing themselves in front of you shamelessly, like offensive linemen setting up a running play.

Joke from Johnny Carson: Married men live longer than single men. But married men are a lot more willing to die.

The smart thing to do (here's some good free advice): Die before she does. It's simpler. You'll be missed. Let everyone else clean up your mess. You won't outlive all your friends. If you predecease your wife, death will hold no surprises for you. You'll still be waiting for her to get ready.

AFTERLIFE

"The secret of a happy marriage remains a secret."
—HENNY YOUNGMAN

In the end, if you have a choice between lucky and smart, choose lucky. Your head, your heart, and your dick are equally unreliable in choosing the right mate for life. It's really a roll of the dice, a crap shoot. Once you've made your choice, and after she's chosen you, all you can do is hope for the best. Then it's up to the two of you and God and fate.

Whatever. A successful marriage is something of a mirage, even after all these years, all this analysis, all the lurid talk shows, and all these goddamn books. Put all the elements together— romance, compatibility, shared interests, love, honor, everything— and, as William Goldman once said about the movie business: "Nobody knows anything."

Hope you guess right with your wife. She has about a million different parts to her, and you'll be lucky if you can figure out any of them.

Hope you guess right with your kids most of the time. You will find religion when you have children, because you will pray to God Almighty that nothing bad happens to them. And he will let you down frequently. They'll get sick, they'll get hurt, they'll get into

trouble, they'll drive you nuts. They'll be all right. The kids are all right.

The old bromide says "The cure for love is marriage and the cure for marriage is love again." When all else fails, love is your fallback position. It's all you've got. And luck.

WHY ME?

"The majority of husbands remind me of
an orangutan trying to play the violin."
—HONORÉ DE BALZAC

Why me? Why should I, as of this writing still, remarkably, unmarried, be the one to write the definitive book about the subject for men? It's a fair question. As Claudette Colbert said after her stroke, "Why not me?" Indeed, why not Me? There is the Melville theory, which states that, by this standard, only a whale could write *Moby-Dick*.[1] This is not *Moby-Dick*, as any literate person will tell you, and neither am I a whale. However, through careful observation and study I can guess right most of the time, and that's what really matters. This is how Dr. Freud operated. And priests.

There are hundreds of books written by and for women, covering every aspect of romantic relationships, mostly how to deal with a certain kind of dysfunctional man. There is some dopey book for almost everything. They are in their own section of the store that men don't visit, with titles like *The Official Book of Flirting; How to Meet Men as Smart as You; Getting to "I Do"; What Do I Have to Give Up to Be with You; Maybe He's Just a Jerk; Smart Women, Foolish Choices; Adultery, the Forgivable Sin; Can This Marriage Be Saved?;* ad infinitum all the way through *Good Divorces, Bad Divorces* and *Joint*

Custody with a Jerk. These women are arming themselves for battle and we're over in the sports section, oblivious to the whole thing.

A few of these books might be somewhat helpful to men, but there is no way in hell you would ever pick up one of these things, much less buy it and be seen in public with it. Many of these books are pink or lavender, some are adorned with hearts. It's very embarrassing. You would rather be caught coming out of a peep show with a copy of *Kiddie Porn* magazine under your arm than have your friends know you are no longer a man. It's true, you technically have to hand over your penis when you buy one of these books. Ask for a plain brown paper bag.

Some of these smarty-pants authors are doctors, which confers a certain degree of authority to whatever half-baked notion they offer up to the massively insecure readers of self-help books. Do you know what they call the person who graduates at the bottom of his class in med school? "Doctor." Although I'm not a doctor, I have spent literally hours reading and researching this stuff so that you don't have to.

If there is a book by and for men, for these lost souls venturing alone into the wilderness, no one knew about it. It seems time that somebody put this whole marriage deal under the microscope and explain it all in simple sentences we simple creatures can all understand.

I do not rely solely on statistical data, culled from extensive surveys, as does Shere Hite. Neither do I merely hypothesize about the nature of things after years of graduate school and hands-on clinical work with target groups, as do so many of my colleagues. It is for others to postulate, extrapolate, and theorize based on carefully documented research on the subject—the so-called facts, which are too often twisted to fit some preconceived hypothesis. They're just in it for the filthy lucre, my friends.

I, on the other hand, have taken a different approach in my quest for the pure and unvarnished truth. I have developed a radically new methodology which, I am confident, will become the model for all future work on the subject: I talked to my friend, whom we shall call "Murray." I went to his wedding and have observed him in his marriage. I have been paying very close attention. Once in a while I might call him up to ask a question or two, but then I guessed at the rest. Journalists who rely merely on "facts" are weak. It shows a lack of scholarly certitude if you must produce footnotes, appendices, a lengthy bibliography, ad nauseam. Einstein did not list a single reference in his landmark paper on the theory of relativity, and neither will I. (Okay, one.)

Besides which, it is unethical to derive your source material from patients who have paid $150 per hour, then blab their stories all over the place for posterity. Instead, when "Murray" shares his wisdom with me, I buy the drinks, thus removing any conflict of interest. Although I have no medical proof of this, it seems that Absolut with a splash of cranberry juice seems to make a man wiser and more insightful.

As if you needed further proof of my qualifications, I hope to get married myself someday soon and test these theories firsthand. I don't see any of the alleged "Doctors" taking up the gauntlet as do I. I'm willing to put my money where my mouth is. That's what separates me and this book—which has already been compared favorably to Freud, *Moby-Dick,* and the theory of relativity—from the others.

That, and the fact that no Married Man's wife would ever let him write this book.

1. This is my only footnote in the book, so pay attention. "Yes," I can hear you saying, "but *Moby-Dick* is fiction." An excellent point. The line between real life (nonfiction) and *Seinfeld* (fiction) has grown increasingly narrow in recent years. So, too, the line between fiction and nonfiction. Al Franken's book *Rush Limbaugh Is a Big Fat Idiot* is in the nonfiction section, while Karen Salmansohn's *How to Succeed in Business Without a Penis* is in the fiction section. You can make the argument that Rush Limbaugh is, in fact, a big fat idiot; and that the idea of a person succeeding in business without a penis is clearly a work of fiction bordering on fantasy; but they are both essentially books of commentary based on personal observations. Humorous observation is the gray area between subjective fiction and objective nonfiction, between your life and *Seinfeld.* There is stuff in this book you might not think is funny now, but it will be when it happens to you (or vice versa). I feel your pain in advance. This is not a self-help book, but if I can inadvertently help just one person it will all have been worthwhile. Does that answer your question?

ACKNOWLEDGMENTS

I hate acknowledgments. It's the worst page in any book. I sometimes find myself halfway down the acknowledgments page and realize it's just pure bullshit. It has nothing to do with me, nothing to do with the contents of the book, nothing to do with anything. Wasted ink, like some rapper giving "props" in "shout outs" to his homeboys.

For most authors it is truly a national ass-kissing forum, probably the only one they'll ever get. There are no "I'd like to thank the Academy" speeches in our future. The Pulitzer Prize awards ceremony isn't televised and, really, who gives a shit?

Having said that, here's the short list of people I owe one to: Marcus Peterzell, without whom . . . , Rob McMahon, Yuri Skujins, Peter Miller, The Steak Club for letting me practice on them; my parents, Julie, Christopher, Danny Fields, Duffy, Carrie & Russ, Claudine, Barry Weiner, the Wylers, Sabols, Kramers, and Backers. Enough, already. Who cares?